Bible Workbook

VOLUME I
Old Testament

Catherine B. Walker

M.A. in Biblical Education, Doctor of Religious Education

MOODY PUBLISHERS
CHICAGO

ACKNOWLEDGMENTS

I wish to express my appreciation for helpful notes and ideas to the Rev. Frank Sells, Miss Louise Tucker, Miss Rachel McAllister, Miss Agnes Stokes, and Miss Margaret Stem. To the great host of Bible teachers and authors who directly or indirectly have added to this book by their contribuion to my own Christian life and Bible knowledge, I am most thankful. To Miss Sara Petty, who from her broad experience has offered such constructive help especially in this work of revision and of checking the manuscript, I am deeply grateful. To the Rev. Byron M. Wilkinson I am indebted for the excellent cartographic work.

BIBLE WORKBOOKS

Volume 1—Old Testament
(A chronological study)

Volume 2—New Testament
(A brief study of all the books)

✈✈✈✈✈✈✈

All Scripture quotations are taken from the King James Version.

Cover and interior design: Erik M. Peterson
Cover engraving, "Moses Coming Down from Mt. Sinai" (1891) by Gustave Dore. Public domain.

ISBN: 978–0–8024–0751–1

We hope you enjoy this book from Moody Publishers. Our goal is to provide high-quality, thought-provoking books and products that connect truth to your real needs and challenges. For more information on other books and products written and produced from a biblical perspective, go to www.moodypublishers.com or write to:

Moody Publishers
820 N. LaSalle Boulevard
Chicago, IL 60610

65 67 69 70 68 66

Printed in the United States of America

NOTE TO THE TEACHER

A need was felt in many high school Bible classes for a method of giving notes and assignment questions quickly, thereby leaving more of the valuable classroom time for explanations, discussions, and student participation. This workbook was first compiled to meet that need. This workbook has also been used by various age groups in churches and colleges and by individuals desiring a better understanding of God's Word.

This is in no sense a textbook. It is hoped that no one will make the completion of the workbook a goal in itself but that the questions and notes may stimulate and guide each student in searching and knowing the Bible. The workbook is planned for a high school course which meets every day for a semester. The workbook has been effectively used in weekly adult Bible classes by dividing it into four units of twelve lessons each, the units starting on pages 4, 25, 47, and 59 respectively. Because of this limited time in which to cover the Old Testament the problem of what to assign for reading and what to omit looms large. By the name of each book or by the questions on the book there are listed suggestive chapters for reading.

The plan of the course is to study Israel's history chronologically. David's and Solomon's writings are fitted in with their lives and the prophets mentioned as they appear in the history of the nation. The course is so arranged as to be flexible according to the individual teacher's emphasis. Some may wish to end their course without completing the Old Testament history but most teachers feel that a brief glance at the whole is profitable in giving the students a rounded view of God's dealing with His chosen people.

This book is not primarily for teachers but for students. It is factual rather than inspirational. The spiritual presentation of the course has been left for each individual teacher to present according to the daily needs of the class. It is hoped that the facts and questions may furnish a basis for making many vital applications of the Old Testament to present-day living.

The notebook may be placed in a regulation size binder so that the separate pages may be handed in when completed. Other notes, assigned papers, and themes can be placed throughout the notebook.

In this second revision, the sections on the kingdom period and the poetic books have been enlarged. The place of Christ in the Old Testament, especially in prophecy, has been set forth more clearly. There are additional notes in the material bringing one's attention to the progressive unfolding of God's plan of redemption.

The following words from 1 Timothy 4:12–16 were sent to me at the beginning of my work of Bible teaching. May the stimulation this passage must have been years ago to Timothy, and more recently to myself, be yours also.

"Let no man despise thy youth; but be thou an example of the believers, in word, in conversation, in charity, in spirit, in faith, in purity. Till I come, give attendance to reading, to exhortation, to doctrine. Neglect not the gift that is in thee, which was given thee by prophecy, with the laying on of the hands of the presbytery. Meditate upon these things; give thyself wholly to them; that thy profiting may appear to all. Take heed unto thyself, and unto the doctrine; continue in them: for in doing this thou shalt both save thyself, and them that hear thee."

Catherine B. Walker

THE WONDERS OF THE BIBLE

The Bible is more wonderful than other books in its:

1. **ORIGIN AND CONSTRUCTION.** No one man or group of men planned the Bible. It was written in different lands over a period of 1600 years. The very existence of such a book is an overwhelming proof that the Bible is not of man, but that it is a production of God. "Holy men of God spake as they were moved by the Holy Ghost." 2 Peter 1:21

2. **UNITY.** The Bible is one great book with one great theme, though it contains 66 separate volumes written by about 40 authors, in three different languages, upon different topics, and under different circumstances. The close fitting together of these varied books into one great book proves someone directed the writing of each and planned the whole. Who could possibly have done it but God?

3. **CIRCULATION.** The Bible, the first book to be printed (AD 1450), is the best seller of the day. The American Bible Society reports more than 287 million Bibles or Bible sections have been distributed worldwide. The circulation of other books is computed in the thousands, the Bible by millions.

4. **AGE NOT AFFECTING ITS PRESENT-DAY APPEAL.** The Bible is not the oldest book, but though the first part of it was written more than 3,000 years ago and the last part nearly 2,000 years ago, today it is more popular than any modern book just off the press.

5. **TRANSLATIONS.** The Bible has been translated into more languages and dialects than any other book. By 1994, the whole Bible had been translated into 347 languages and the New Testament into 822. At least one or more of the Bible books can be read in 2,092 of the world's estimated 6,000 languages.

6. **INTEREST FOR ALL CLASSES OF PEOPLE.** Old, young, rich, poor, wise, simple, high, and low are all gripped by the appeal of the Bible.

7. **INEXHAUSTIBLE MEANING.** Though anyone can easily understand its main message, the most brilliant minds cannot fully understand its deepest thoughts. The highest intellect cannot completely grasp all its meaning. Great volumes have been written on single verses.

8. **STIMULATION TO ART, LITERATURE, MUSIC, ETC.**

    Many of the world's masterpieces and movements have been motivated by the Bible.

    > Literature–Milton's *Paradise Lost*, Bunyan's *Pilgrim's Progress*.
    > Art—*The Last Supper* by DeVinci.
    > Music—*The Messiah* by Handel.
    > Architecture—St. Peter's Cathedral.
    > Movements in history—The Reformation, Missions, Education, Social Reform.

9. **CLAIM TO BE GOD'S WORD.** More than 2,000 times in the Old Testament, the words "thus saith the Lord" or similar terms are used. No other book matches such claims. Anyone who reads the Bible with open mind and heart is convinced that the Bible is God's word to man.

10. **PROPHECIES.** The Bible records the most unlikely predictions concerning the future, yet at the appointed time they happen and the Bible then records the fulfillments. Notice how Micah 5:2 was fulfilled hundreds of years later. See Matt. 2:4–6.

11. **SURVIVAL OF PERSECUTION.** History shows that mighty kings, emperors, and priests have tried at times to destroy this book. They have died but the Bible lives on. Wycliffe and Tyndale were persecuted because they translated the Bible. Other men and women have died rather than deny the Bible and the Christ it presents.

    The Bible has also suffered the blows of men who have taught that it was not inspired of God but was full of human errors. These men pass away but the Bible continues.

12. **CENTRAL CHARACTER.** The main character of the Bible is Jesus Christ. He is the greatest wonder of the Bible. No other religion offers a living Savior.

THINGS FOR YOU TO DO:

Bring to class any of the following:
1. The statement of some famous man about the Bible.
2. Some Old Testament prophecy which has been fulfilled.
3. A translation of the Bible into some language other than English.
4. Some piece of music, art, or literature which was inspired by the Bible.

INTRODUCTION TO THE BIBLE

I. **THEME OR SUBJECT:** a history of God's plan for the redemption of man from sin through Christ.
   Note throughout the course the references to people and events connected with the development of this plan.

II. **NAMES:**
   A. Bible: The word comes from a Latin and a Greek word meaning "book" or "books."
   B. Word of God.
   C. Scriptures: The word means "writings." Before the time of the printing press copies were written by hand.

III. **COMPARISONS:**
   To what does the Bible compare itself?
   Jeremiah 23:29 _____
   Jeremiah 23:29 _____
   James 1:23–25 _____
   Ephesians 5:26 _____
   Luke 8:11 _____
   Psalm 119:105 _____
   Ephesians 6:17 _____
   1 Peter 2:2 _____
   Jeremiah 15:16 _____
   Psalm 19:10 _____
   Psalm 19:10 _____

IV. **AUTHOR AND AUTHORS:** God through men.
   About 36 to 40 holy men were moved by the Holy Spirit to write exactly what God wanted written.
   Memorize 2 Peter 1:21 and 2 Timothy 3:16–17.
   Name nine men you believe wrote parts of the Bible.

   1. _____   4. _____   7. _____
   2. _____   5. _____   8. _____
   3. _____   6. _____   9. _____

V. **BIBLE DIVISIONS:**
   Old Testament
      3   9 = 39 books in the Old Testament
   New Testament
      3 x 9 = 27 books in the New Testament
          ———
          66 books in the entire Bible.

VI. **OLD TESTAMENT DIVISIONS AND BOOKS**
   Learn the divisions and names of the Old Testament books in order.
   (The five divisions can quickly be learned by associating them with the five fingers. Let the thumb represent the five books of the Laws, etc.)

Law (Pentateuch)	5	Genesis, Exodus, Leviticus, Numbers, Deuteronomy
History	12	Joshua, Judges, Ruth, 1 and 2 Samuel, 1 and 2 Kings, 1 and 2 Chronicles, Ezra, Nehemiah, Esther

Poetry	5	Job, Psalms, Proverbs, Ecclesiastes, Song of Solomon
Major Prophets	5	Isaiah, Jeremiah, Lamentations, Ezekiel, Daniel
Minor Prophets	12	Hosea, Joel, Amos, Obadiah, Jonah, Micah, Nahum, Habakkuk, Zephaniah, Haggai, Zechariah, Malachi

(The major prophetic books are larger than the minor ones.)

VII. GENERAL OUTLINE OF HEBREW HISTORY (*Learn*)

1. Introduction: Creation, Fall, Flood, Nations
2. The Period of the Patriarchs: Abraham, Isaac, Jacob, and Joseph
3. The Going out of Egypt into Canaan: Moses, Aaron, and Joshua
4. The Dark Ages: Judges
5. The United Kingdom: Saul, David, and Solomon
6. The Divided Kingdom: Judah and Israel
7. The Captivity
8. The Restoration

VIII. TYPES OF LITERATURE IN THE BIBLE (with examples)

History_____ Genesis	Prophecy _____ Isaiah
Poetry _____ Psalms	Letters _____ 1 Timothy
Biography _____ Mark	Drama _____ Job
Philosophy _____ Ecclesiastes	Romance_____ Ruth

IX. ORIGINAL FORM:

Parts of the Bible originally were written probably on stone, clay tablets, papyrus, sheepskin, and scrolls.

X. DATES

The Bible was written over a period of sixteen centuries:

Genesis	1600 years	Revelation
Moses–1500 BC		John—100 AD

XI. ORIGINAL LANGUAGES:

The Old Testament was written in Hebrew (with a few chapters in Aramaic).
The New Testament was written in Greek.

XII. OLDEST MANUSCRIPTS: ("Manuscript" means "written by hand")

None of the original manuscripts of Moses, David, Paul, etc., are in existence today.

The oldest copies of the Bible today were made from other copies of the original. The three oldest, most complete, hand-written copies of the Bible are:

THE ALEXANDRIAN MANUSCRIPT, which was once a part of the great library in Alexandria, Egypt, and now is in the British Museum.

THE VATICAN MANUSCRIPT, which was found and remains in the library of Vatican City, Rome, Italy.

THE SINAITIC MANUSCRIPT, which was found by Count Tischendorf in the wastebaskets in St. Catherine's Convent at the foot of Mt. Sinai. Though first placed in the library at St. Petersburg, Russia, it is now in the British Museum.

None of these ancient manuscripts had been found when the King James Authorized Version was translated in 1611.

XIII. FAMOUS VERSIONS OF THE BIBLE: ("Version" means "translation")

A. **THE SEPTUAGINT** is called the Bible of the LXX because tradition says that in the third century BC seventy men took seventy days to translate the Hebrew Old Testament into Greek. This version of the Old Testament was used by Jesus and His disciples.

B. **THE LATIN VULGATE** is a translation of the entire Bible into Latin by Saint Jerome about AD 400. It was the only Bible the English possessed for centuries. The first Bibles in the English language were translations of this Latin Bible rather than from the original Hebrew and Greek.

C. **JOHN WYCLIFFE** was the first to translate the Bible into English, in 1382. Copies of it were made by hand because printing was not invented until 1450 Wycliffe was cast out of the church (excommunicated) and his translation condemned because he had made the Bible available to the Englishman in his own language.

D. **WILLIAM TYNDALE** in 1525 made a more accurate translation into English from the original Hebrew and Greek. Printed copies of this Bible soon poured into England. For this, by order of the church, Tyndale was burned at the stake.

E. **THE KING JAMES AUTHORIZED VERSION** was translated in 1611 by order of King James I of England. Fifty-four scholars compared all the manuscripts available before translating this work. This still is the version most familiar to the English-speaking people everywhere.

F. **AMERICAN REVISED VERSION** is a revision of the King James version made by eighty-three English and American scholars begun in 1870. This was needed because of the change in the meaning of some of the older English words and because of the discovery of more accurate ancient manuscripts. (See Oldest Manuscripts.)

G. **THE REVISED STANDARD VERSION OF THE NEW TESTAMENT** appeared in 1946 and the RSV Old Testament in 1952.

H. **WEYMOUTH, MOFFATT, GOODSPEED, WILLIAMS** and others in recent years have made translations of the Bible into modern speech. The NEW INTERNATIONAL VERSION was completed in 1978.

(The chapter and verse divisions are not inspired and were not in the original writings. In 1236 the chapters were divided and in 1551 Robert Stephens made the verse divisions.)

XIV. YOU AND YOUR STUDY OF THE OLD TESTAMENT

1. *Become familiar with the contents of each book.*
2. *Learn the outline or the outstanding themes.*
3. *As you read underline the verses that you like. Memorizing many of these will aid in your spiritual growth.*
4. *Watch God as He works through men and events to prepare for the coming of Christ.*
5. *The men and women you meet in the Bible were human beings subject to the same feelings and experiences that you know today. Watch God as He changes men and meets the need of each individual.*
6. *In each lesson expect to hear God's still small voice saying some of the things to you He has said to men of old. As the Chinese boy says, "Believe the Bible and behave it."*

GENESIS

NAME: "Genesis" is a Greek word meaning "beginning." The book tells of the beginning of everything except God who is without beginning or end.

AUTHOR: Moses

DATE: 1500 BC Moses lived about as far on the other side of Christ as Columbus, who discovered America, lived on this side of Christ.

OUTLINE: *(Learn)*

    A. History of the human race (Gen. 1–11)
1. Creation
2. Fall
3. Flood
4. Tower of Babel (Nations)

    B. History of the chosen race, the Jews (Gen. 12–50)
1. Abraham
2. Isaac
3. Jacob
4. Joseph

	Human Race	Abraham and the Chosen Race		
Genesis	ch. 1 to ch. 11	ch. 12	to	ch. 50
	2000 years (?)		315 years	

HISTORY OF THE HUMAN RACE—GENESIS 1–11
CREATION (GENESIS 1–2)

Genesis 1 outlines creation as a whole

Genesis 2 retells creation especially emphasizing man's place

I. THE CREATOR

    A. *List what you discover about God from these chapters*

        1. _____
        2. _____
        3. _____
        4. _____
        5. _____
        6. _____

    B. The Bible reveals God as a "trinity" (one God yet three persons), God the F_____, God the S_____, and God the Holy _____.

        Notice the pronouns in Genesis 1:26.

        Which person in the Godhead is mentioned in Genesis 1:2?_____

        Was the Son of God present in creation?_____ (Read John 1:1–3; Col. 1:16).

II. THE CREATION

    A. The word "create," meaning to make out of nothing, is used three times in Genesis 1.

        Genesis 1:1   God created matter (the material universe)

        Genesis 1:21   God created animal life

        Genesis 1:27   God created human life

    B. *Name in order what God did each of the days of creation week:*

        1st day _____   5th day _____

        2nd day_____   6th day _____

        3rd day _____   7th day _____

        4th day_____

C. Which day did God bless and sanctify? (2:1–3) _____

D. How long do you think these days were? _____

E. What does "after his kind" mean in Genesis 1:11, 12, 21, 24?_____

_____

F. Have you known any other explanation for the creation of the world? _____

(In your thinking and reading, distinguish between the proved FACTS of science and the unproved THEORIES.)

Professor Dana said of this first chapter in the Bible, "I find it to be in perfect accord with known science." To a graduating class at Yale he said, "Young men! As you go out into the world to face scientific problems, remember that I, an old man who has known only science all my life long, say to you, that there is nothing truer in all the Universe than the scientific statements contained in the Word of God."

III. CREATION'S CLIMAX—MAN

A. Man's beginning:

1. Of what two things was man created? (2:7) _____

2. In whose image was man made? _____

3. Why did God make man? (Read Isa. 43:7, Rev. 4:11) _____

4. How do we know that God planned for man to work? (2:15) _____

5. Who named the animals and fowls that God made?_____

B. Man's first home: The Garden of _____

1. This garden was probably located in the Mesopotamian plain.

The name of what river is familiar to you? (2:11–14) _____

See the probable location on the map, page 13.

2. In those days how was the earth watered? (2:6) _____

3. What did God give man and animals for food? (1:29–30)_____

4. What two unusual trees were in the garden? 1._____

2. _____

5. What one restriction or test of obedience was given to man? (2:17) _____

_____

(In the garden there was health, happiness, and holiness.)

C. Man's wife: Called _____(2:23),_____(3:20), and_____(5:2)

1. Why was she made? _____

2. How was she made?_____

_____

MAN'S FALL INTO SIN (GENESIS 3–4)

I. WHAT THE BIBLE TEACHES ABOUT SATAN

"That old serpent, called the Devil, and Satan" (Rev. 12:9) apparently was first created as one of the **cherubim** (Ezek. 28:12–15), having great position and authority. He fell from his heavenly estate through his rebellious attitude of **pride** (Isa. 14:12–15).

After the creation of the earth he tempted mankind likewise **to act in self-will** instead of God's will. (Gen. 3:1–6). His **plan is to dethrone God** in His universe and in the hearts of men. God promises **Satan's ultimate destruction** through the "seed of the woman," Christ (Gen. 3:15).

Three times Jesus called him **"the prince of this world"** (John 14:30, etc.). As "the prince of the power of the air" (Eph. 2:2) he heads a vast host of demons. The present world system organized upon the principles of force, greed, selfishness, ambition, and sinful pleasure is his work. In His own time, **God's full judgment will come upon Satan** (Rev. 20:10) and the absolute, undivided sovereignty of God over His whole universe will be restored.

II. TEMPTATION OF ADAM AND EVE

1. What did Satan cause Eve to doubt? _____
   _____

2. How did Satan do this? _____
   _____

3. What are some of the things Satan tempts us to doubt about God? _____
   _____

4. How did Jesus meet Satan's temptations? (Read Luke 4:1–13) _____
   _____

III. THE RESULTS OF SIN

1. For the serpent? (3:14–15) _____
2. For the woman? (3:16) _____
3. For the man? (3:17, 19) _____
4. For the ground? (3:18) _____
5. Has spiritual and physical death resulted from sin?_____
6. How can we escape spiritual death? (Rom. 6:23) _____
   _____

7. How did Adam and Eve try to cover their sin and nakedness? _____
   _____

8. How did God clothe Adam and Eve? _____
9. By driving Adam and Eve from Eden, God, in kindness, kept them away from what? (3:24)
   _____

IV. THE FIRST PROMISE OF A SAVIOR (GENESIS 3:15)

*Quote and memorize*_____
_____
_____
_____

V CAIN AND ABEL

1. Why was God pleased with Abel's offering? (Heb. 11:4)_____
   _____

2. *List all of Cain's sins in the order they occurred* _____
   _____
   _____

3. Whom do you think Cain married?_____
4. What were the occupations of the early descendants of Cain? (4:20–22) _____
   _____

5. What son was given to Adam and Eve to take Abel's place? _____

VI. WHAT THE BIBLE TEACHES ABOUT SIN

(Memorize as assigned by the teacher)

A. What is sin?
   1 John 3:4 "Sin is the_____"
   John 16:7–9 "The Comforter . . . will reprove the world of sin . . . because they_____
   _____ on me (Jesus)."

10

B. Who has sinned?

Romans 3:23 "_____ have sinned."

Isaiah 53:6 "_____we like_____have gone astray; we have turned every one to_____

_____ _____ ”

C. Consequences of sin:

Romans 6:23 " _____ _____of sin is _____."

John 3:36 "He that believeth on the Son hath everlasting life: and he that believeth not the Son

_____ _____ _____ _____; but the _____ _____

_____ abideth on him."

Revelation 20:15 "And whosoever was not found written in the book of life was _____into

the _____ _____ _____.”

D. Provision for forgiveness:

John 3:16 "For God so _____ the _____ that he _____ his only

begotten _____, that whosoever _____ _____ _____should not

_____, but have everlasting _____."

1 John 1:7 "The _____of Jesus Christ his Son _____us from _____."

Also see 2 Peter 3:9, Hebrews 9:22, 26, 28; Isaiah 53:5, 6; 1 John 2:2; Galatians 3:13.

E. Conditions of forgiveness:

John 1:12 "But as many as _____Him (Jesus), to them gave he power to become the

_____ _____ _____, even to them that _____ on his name."

1 John 1:9 "If we _____ _____ _____, he is faithful and just to

forgive us our sins, and to_____us from _____ unrighteousness."

Also see Romans 10:9, 10; Revelation 3:20; Matthew 7:13, 14; John 3:7.

F. When can one be saved?

2 Corinthians 6:2 "_____, _____ _____ the day of salvation."

Proverbs 27:1 "Boast not thyself of _____; for _____ _____ _____

what a day may bring forth."

G. Can one know he is saved?

1 John 5:13 "These things have I _____ unto you that believe on the name of the Son of

God; that ye may _____ _____ _____ _____ _____ _____,

and that ye _____ _____ _____ _____ _____ of the Son of God."

THE FLOOD (GENESIS 5–9)

1. How old was Adam when he died? (5:5)_____

2. Who is the oldest man in this chapter and in the Bible? (5:27)_____

3. Who walked with God and did not die? (5:24) _____

4. Why did God decide to destroy man? (6:5) _____

_____

5. *Describe Noah:*_____

_____

6. The ark was to be made of _____wood, _____ cubits long, _____

cubits broad, and _____ cubits high, with _____ stories, a window, and a door.

William Matthew Petrie gives the ancient cubit as equal to 22.5". This would make the ark 562' 6" long by 93' 9" wide by 56' 3" high with 2,958,000 cubic feet of space, which equals the carrying load of 1,000 freight cars. The ark was six times long as it was wide. Some of the finest ships afloat are built in proportion to the ark.

7. How many of each clean animal were taken into the ark? (7:2) _____

8. How many of each unclean animal were taken into the ark? _____

9. Who were the eight people in the ark? _____

_____

10. How long did it rain? _____

11. On what mountain did the ark rest? (8:4) _____

12. What two birds were sent out of the ark to test whether the water was down? _____
_____

13. What did Noah do immediately after he left the ark? _____
_____

After reading Genesis 6–8 write a short story, or letter, or diary, or news report telling about the flood, pretending you were one of Noah's family. Use vivid, reverent imagination.

Noah's household were in the ark 1 year and 17 days, as follows:

    7 days in the ark before the rain began

  40 days it rained day and night

110 days more, the ark rested on Mt. Ararat

 73 days more, the mountain tops were visible

 40 days more, Noah sent out a raven

   7 days more, Noah sent out a dove; it returned

   7 days more, Noah sent out another dove; it returned

   7 days more, Noah sent out another dove; it did not return

 29 days more, the covering of the ark was removed

 57 days more, Noah went out of the ark

14. What did God now give man for food? (9:3)_____

15. Did God ever command capital punishment? (9:6) _____

16. What is the meaning of the rainbow? _____
_____

ORIGIN OF NATIONS (GENESIS 10–11)

GENESIS 10–DESCENDANTS FROM NOAH'S SONS

Shem's descendants settled chiefly in Central Asia.

Ham's descendants settled chiefly in Africa.

Japheth's descendants settled chiefly in Europe.

GENESIS 11–TOWER OF BABEL

1. Why did the people want to build the Tower of Babel? (11:4)_____
_____

2. How did the Lord stop the building of the tower? _____
_____

3. *Locate the Tower of Babel. It was probably near the Babylon of later years. See the map, page 13.*

HISTORY OF THE CHOSEN RACE—GENESIS 12–50

THE PLAN OF REDEMPTION

As the events of the Old Testament progress there is the continuous development of God's plan to bring into the world the Redeemer through the chosen race, Israel, in the chosen land, Palestine. *Notice how the lives of Abraham, Isaac, Jacob, and Joseph are connected with this plan of redemption.*

THE PURPOSE OF HAVING ONE CHOSEN RACE WAS:

1. To keep alive the worship of the one true God.
2. To illustrate to other nations the blessedness of serving the true God.
3. To receive and preserve God's Word, the Bible.
4. To give birth to the Messiah, Jesus Christ.

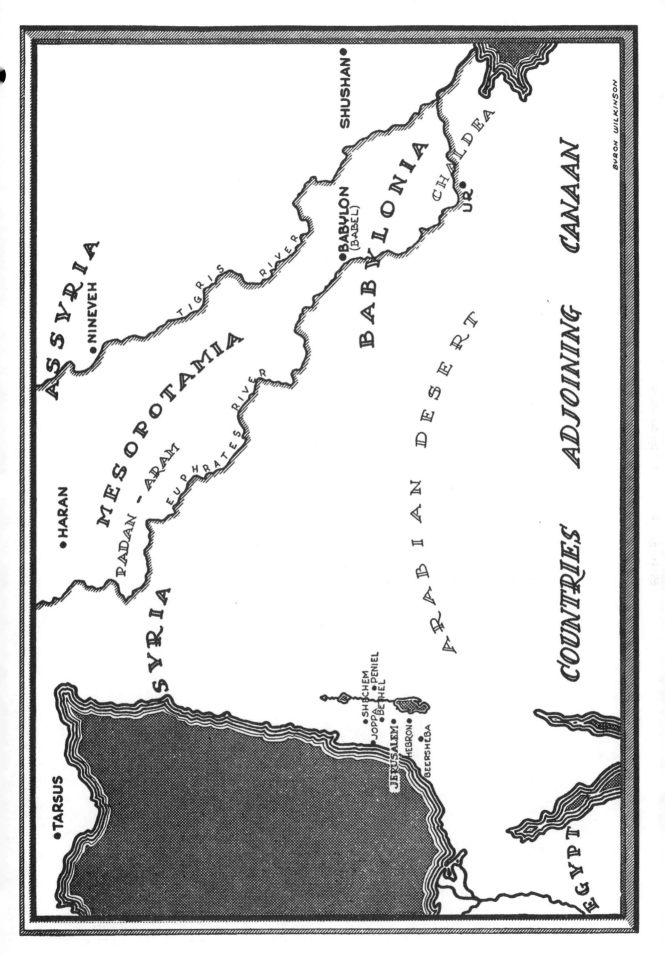

CANAAN
AND
ADJOINING
COUNTRIES

BYRON WILKINSON

ASSYRIA
NINEVEH

MESOPOTAMIA
HARAN
PADAN - ARAM

TIGRIS RIVER
EUPHRATES RIVER

BABYLON
(BABEL)

BABYLONIA

CHALDEA
UR

SHUSHAN

ARABIAN DESERT

SYRIA
TARSUS

SHECHEM
PENIEL
BETHEL
JOPPA
JERUSALEM
HEBRON
BEERSHEBA

EGYPT

THE FATHER OF THE CHOSEN RACE—ABRAHAM

Date: Abraham lived about 2000 B.C.

Adam	Abraham	Christ	Today
4000 BC	2000 BC		AD 2000

Hammurabi was living at the same time as Abraham. *Use a reference material to find out who Hammurabi was* _____

_____

_____

Honor: Abraham is today honored by:

JEWS as the father and founder of the Hebrew race.

CHRISTIANS as the father of all who believe God. (Gal. 3:6–9, 29)

MUSLIMS as the father of Ishmael.

Abraham is called _____. (James 2:23)

Family tree:

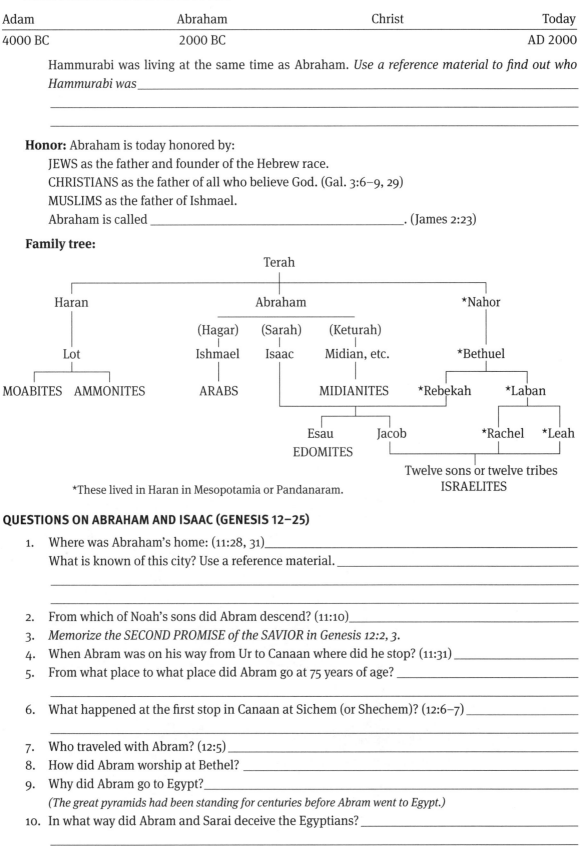

*These lived in Haran in Mesopotamia or Pandanaram.

QUESTIONS ON ABRAHAM AND ISAAC (GENESIS 12–25)

1. Where was Abraham's home: (11:28, 31)_____
   What is known of this city? Use a reference material. _____

   _____

   _____

2. From which of Noah's sons did Abram descend? (11:10)_____

3. *Memorize the SECOND PROMISE of the SAVIOR in Genesis 12:2, 3.*

4. When Abram was on his way from Ur to Canaan where did he stop? (11:31) _____

5. From what place to what place did Abram go at 75 years of age? _____

   _____

6. What happened at the first stop in Canaan at Sichem (or Shechem)? (12:6–7) _____

   _____

7. Who traveled with Abram? (12:5) _____

8. How did Abram worship at Bethel? _____

9. Why did Abram go to Egypt?_____

   (The great pyramids had been standing for centuries before Abram went to Egypt.)

10. In what way did Abram and Sarai deceive the Egyptians? _____

    _____

11. To what place did Abram return to build an altar and worship? (13:3–4)_____

12. Why did Abram and Lot separate?_____
_____

13. What did Lot choose? (13:11–12) _____

14. What kind of people lived in Sodom? _____

15. What marvelous promise did God make to Abram? (13:14–17) _____
_____
_____
_____

16. In what town did Abram finally settle? (13:18) H_____ in the plains of M_____

17. *Trace Abram's journeys from Ur here. See the map, page 13.*

18. When four kings fought against five kings what relative of Abram's was captured? (14:1–16)
_____

19. Aside from his confederates, how many in Abram's own army of trained servants went with him
to rescue the captives? (14:14) _____

20. What did Melchizedek do for Abram? (14:18–20) _____
_____

21. What did Abram give Melchizedek? T_____, a word which means_____
(Read Hebrews 7 and find who is compared to Melchizedek in the New Testament. Notice verse 22.)

22. What did the rich man Abram lack and want? (15:3) _____

23. The vision in Genesis 15 was to prove to Abraham that God would keep his promise. What did God
say would happen to Abraham's seed some day? (15:13–16) _____
_____

24. What happened to Hagar? (16) _____
_____
_____

25. When Abram was _____ years old God made a _____with him. His name
was changed to _____, which means _____
He promised him the land of _____ as an _____
possession. God promised Abraham a son, _____by his wife, _____
who was then _____ years old. Her name was changed to _____, which means
"princess." The covenant was to be with Abraham's son, _____, not with
_____. The sign of this covenant was circumcision. (17)

26. What message did the heavenly visitors bring Abraham? (18) _____
_____

27. Did Sarah laugh at this news in a spirit of belief or unbelief? (18:10–15)_____

28. Why did Abraham want God to spare Sodom from punishment?_____
_____

29. Did the people of Sodom believe God would destroy their city? (19:14) _____

30. Who did escape from Sodom? (19:16) _____

31. Why did Lot's wife become a pillar of salt? (19:17, 26)_____
_____

32. Sodom is known as "the filthiest city of antiquity." Did the filth of Sodom cling to Lot's family?

33. *Name three things you admire about Abraham.* _____
_____
_____

34. *Name three things you dislike in Lot.* _____
_____
_____

35. What happened to Hagar and Ishmael after Isaac's birth? (21) _____

_____

_____

36. God told Abraham to take _____ to Mt. _____ and _____.
    After the test Abraham did offer a _____ found _____ (22)

37. What had God said about Isaac which would make it especially hard for Abraham to understand this command? (17:19) _____

_____

    Abraham had such faith in this promise that he believed God would raise Isaac from the dead if necessary. *(Read Hebrews 11:17–19).*

38. What was the purpose of God's asking Abraham to sacrifice Isaac? _____

_____

39. *List several ways in which Abraham's offering Isaac was like God's offering Jesus at Calvary:*

_____

_____

_____

40. What cave in Hebron did Abraham buy for a burial place? (23) _____

41. Whom did he bury there? _____

42. What did Abraham consider a most important step in his son's career? (24) _____

_____

43. *Be able to tell accurately the story, "How Rebekah Was Found" (24). Study the chart on page 15. From studying the story and the characteristics of Isaac and Rebekah give some discoveries as to the essentials of a happy or successful marriage.* _____

_____

_____

_____

44. Where was Abraham buried at 175 years of age? (25:7–10) _____

45. *Have you completed tracing Abraham's journeys on page 13?* _____

QUESTIONS ON ISAAC AND JACOB—(GENESIS 25–36)

1. What do you admire about Jacob? _____

_____

2. What do you dislike in Jacob? _____

_____

3. What do you admire about Esau? _____

_____

4. What do you dislike in Esau? _____

_____

5. *Be able to tell the story, "Jacob Gets Esau's Birthright" (25:27–34)*
   Having the birthright meant:
   a. Being head of the family or tribe.
   b. Receiving material possessions—receiving double portion of his father's property.
   c. Receiving spiritual blessings—receiving the promises given to Abraham and becoming the ancestor of Christ.

6. How did Jacob steal Esau's blessing? (27) _____

_____

_____

_____

_____

7. The name "Jacob" means "supplanter" or "trickster." How many times did he live up to his name? (27:36) _____

8. Why did Jacob plan to flee to his relatives in Haran?_____

_____

9. When Jacob fled from home, was he ready in character and spirit to be the father of the twelve tribes, God's chosen race? _____

10. Put yourself in Jacob's place at Bethel. What did Jacob learn about God there? _____

_____

_____

_____

11. What promise was repeated to Jacob? (28:13–14) _____

_____

_____

12. In what two ways did Laban deceive Jacob? (29) 1. _____

_____

(31:7) 2. _____

_____

13. How did Jacob's experience illustrate the verse "Whatsoever a man soweth, that shall he also reap?" Galatians 6:7_____

_____

_____

14. Since Jacob's mother, Rebekah, had not sent for him, why was Jacob going to return to Canaan? (31) *(Review 27:43–45)* _____

15. How did Jacob leave? (31) _____
    Why? _____

16. How long had Jacob been in Haran working? (31:38–41) _____

17. Why was Jacob afraid to meet Esau? (32:1–11) _____

_____

18. What various things did Jacob do when he heard that Esau was coming? _____

_____

_____

_____

19. At Peniel that night, the turning point in Jacob's life took place. He received from God the blessing he had earlier sought to obtain in evil ways. God was wrestling with Jacob to get what quality out of him?_____

Jacob now is a new man with a new name, _____, which means "a prince of God."

20. Can anyone have power with God until he has surrendered to Him? _____

21. How did Esau meet and greet Jacob? (33) _____

_____

22. What preparations were made for Jacob's return to Bethel? (35) _____

_____

23. *List the things about this visit to Bethel that are different from the earlier one. (35:9–15 and 28:10–22)*

_____

_____

_____

_____

24. What three sorrows came to Jacob after coming to Bethel? (35)

1. _____

2. _____

3. _____

25. *Learn the names of Jacob's twelve sons: (35:23–26)*

Grouping the first letters of the names as follows may help in remembering the sons:

RINGS   BALD   JJZ

R_____	B_____	J_____
I_____	A_____	J_____
N_____	L_____	Z_____
G_____	D_____	
S_____		

QUESTIONS ON JACOB AND JOSEPH (GENESIS 37–50)

1. What are three of the reasons that Joseph's brothers hated him? (37)

1. _____

2. _____

3. _____

2. What are the main steps in the story of Joseph's going from his father's house to that of Potiphar in Egypt? (37) _____

_____

_____

_____

_____

_____

3. Which two of Joseph's brothers stood out as leaders? _____

_____

4. How did Jacob reap from his sons the same thing he had sown? _____

5. *List five or six qualities of character that Joseph showed while a slave in Potiphar's house. (39)*

_____

_____

6. What two outstanding characteristics of Joseph are shown while in prison? (39:20–40:23)

_____

7. What had Joseph seen in his two boyhood dreams? (37) _____

_____

_____

_____

8. What had the butler and the baker seen in their two dreams? (40)

    1. Butler _____

    _____

    _____

    2. Baker _____

    _____

9. What did Pharaoh see in his two dreams? (41) _____

_____

_____

_____

_____

10. Why was Joseph offered the place of Prime Minister of Egypt? (41) *(Observe what Pharaoh would have noticed about him.)* _____

_____

_____

_____

11. *Be able to tell exactly what happened on the brothers' first visit to Egypt.*

12. Did Joseph's treatment of his brothers hinder or help in the development of their character?

_____

13. *Live through the brothers' second visit to Egypt with them. Think their thoughts and feel their emotions. Be able to tell the story vividly.*

    The story of Joseph has been called the most dramatic narrative in the Bible. Do you see why?

_____

14. Which brother takes the lead in eloquently pleading for Benjamin? _____

15. In what way have the brothers changed after twenty years or so? _____

_____

16. What happened when Jacob heard that Joseph was alive in Egypt? (45) _____

_____

17. What were God's words to Jacob before he departed for Egypt? (46:1–4) _____

_____

18. In what place, separated from the Egyptians, did this family live? _____

19. During the famine was Joseph a success as a Prime Minister? (47) _____

20. *In looking back over Joseph's life, list some of the things that were similar to the life of Jesus.*

_____

_____

_____

_____

_____

_____

21. Who were Joseph's sons? (48) _____

_____

22. How were they blessed? _____

_____

23. In Jacob's prophecies of his twelve sons, (49:8–12) what kind of person is prophesied to come from Judah's family?_____

24. Where was Jacob buried?_____

25. After his father's death, what was Joseph's attitude toward his brothers and the past happenings? (50:15–21)_____
_____

26. What request did Joseph make concerning his own "bones"? (50:24–26)_____
_____

LOOKING BACK THROUGH GENESIS

GOD IN GENESIS

If you only had the book of Genesis what would you know about God? *List definite ideas.*

_____
_____
_____
_____
_____
_____
_____
_____
_____
_____
_____

THE SON OF GOD IN GENESIS APPEARS:

1. In the visible **appearances** of God. (Sometimes he is called "the angel of the Lord") *Mention three of these appearances:*

   _____
   _____
   _____

2. In **prophecies:**
   a. Genesis 3:15   Christ is the "seed of the woman"
   b. Genesis 22:18   He is the "seed of Abraham"
   c. Genesis 26:4   He is the "seed of Isaac"
   d. Genesis 28:14   He is the "seed of Jacob"
   e. Genesis 49:10   He is the ruler from Judah

3. In **types**:
   Name one character and an event in Genesis you think God planned to be a foreshadowing or picture of a future New Testament event.

O. T. Foreshadowing	N. T. Fulfillment
_____	_____
_____	_____

4. In the history of the chosen race, **Israel:**
   List in order the important people in the line of Christ in Genesis:

   _____
   _____
   _____
   _____

WHO'S WHO IN GENESIS

(Read Hebrews 11:1–22)

Here is a game for class. See if you can recognize all the characters you have met in Genesis.

_____ The first man

_____ The first woman

_____ Adam's oldest son and the first murderer

_____ Adam's righteous son, the first person to die

_____ Adam's son replacing Abel

_____ Walked with God and never died

_____ Oldest man yet died before his father

_____ Built the ark and was saved from the flood

_____ Son of Noah, father of the Hebrews and Arabs

_____ Son of Noah, father of Egyptians and Ethiopians

_____ Son of Noah, father of Greeks and Romans

_____ Father of Abram

_____ Father of the Hebrew race, God's chosen people

_____ Nephew of Abram who chose to live in Sodom

_____ Sarah's handmaid

_____ Son of Abraham and Hagar

_____ Priest of God to whom Abraham paid tithes

_____ Beautiful wife of Abraham

_____ Son of Abraham and Sarah, the child of promise

_____ Abraham's servant who went for a bride for Isaac

_____ Wife of Isaac

_____ Brother of Rebekah, Jacob's uncle

_____ Isaac and Rebekah's son who desired the birthright

_____ Isaac and Rebekah's son who despised the birthright

_____ Laban's eldest daughter, Jacob's wife

_____ Favorite wife of Jacob

_____ Jacob's son through whom the kingly line and Redeemer would come

_____ Jacob's oldest son

_____ Jacob's youngest son

_____ Saved Israel from the famine in Egypt

_____ Captain of the guards in Egypt, bought Joseph

_____ Ruler of Egypt

_____ Joseph's younger son

_____ Joseph's older son

1. Reuben	8. Isaac	15. Adam	22. Manasseh	29. Abraham
2. Lot	9. Jacob	16. Seth	23. Joseph	30. Methuselah
3. Ishmael	10. Leah	17. Ham	24. Abel	31. Esau
4. Melchizedek	11. Judah	18. Terah	25. Pharaoh	32. Rebekah
5. Sarah	12. Ephraim	19. Japheth	26. Enoch	33. Laban
6. Eliezer	13. Potiphar	20. Cain	27. Noah	34. Rachel
7. Hagar	14. Benjamin	21. Eve	28. Shem	

JOB

Read Job 1, 2, 42

LITERARY FORM: A dramatic poem, a literary masterpiece, probably the oldest of the Bible books.

THEME: The problem of human suffering. Why do the godly suffer?

TIME: Job probably lived in the Patriarchal Age between the time of Abraham and Moses.

THINGS FOR YOU TO DO:

I. *Think these questions over before class and write your opinions.*

    1. Who brings suffering and trouble on earth? _____

    2. Who permits these things? _____

    3. What are some of the reasons God allows terrible things to happen? _____

    _____

    _____

    _____

    4. Is human suffering always sent as punishment? (Luke 13:1–5, John 9:1–3) _____

II. *Be able to read as a dialogue the conversation between God and Satan: Job 1:7–12, 2:1–6.*

III. *Answer the following questions:*

    1. Where did Job live? _____

    2. Job had how many sons? _____ How many daughters? _____

    3. Job had how many sheep? _____ camels? _____ yoke of oxen? _____

    4. Why did Job offer burnt offerings for his children? _____

    _____

    5. What kind of a man was Job? (1:1, 2:3) _____

    _____

    6. According to Satan's view why did Job fear and serve God? (1:9–11) _____

    _____

    7. The FIRST TEST of the genuineness of Job's devotion came when God permitted Satan to take away from Job all his earthly possessions.

    Number the following disasters in the order in which they came: (1:13–19)

    _____ camels stolen and servants slain

    _____ sheep and servants killed by fire

    _____ sons and daughters killed

    _____ oxen and asses stolen and servants slain.

    8. Did Job pass this first test? _____ What was Job's answer? (1:20–21) _____

    _____

    _____

    9. The SECOND TEST was on Job's own body. What suffering did Satan bring to Job? _____

    _____

    10. Did Job pass this second test? _____ What was Job's reply? (2:10) _____

    _____

    _____

    11. Genesis, Job, and Revelation give insight into the person and work of Satan. How is the characteristic of Satan shown in Revelation 12:10 illustrated in the life of Job? _____

    _____

(Review notes on Satan, page 9)

12. Summary of arguments in the book of Job.

Job 2 to 31 gives the discussion between Job and his three friends as to why all this trouble has come to Job. The friends, Eliphaz, Bildad, and Zophar say it is the punishment for sin.

In Job 32 to 37 Elihu says suffering is a means of purifying and chastening.

In Job 38 to 41 God Himself shows that if man cannot understand some of the instincts and ways of the created things, he cannot fully understand his Creator and His ways.

13. How did Job's prosperity at the end of his life compare with that at the beginning? _____

_____

14. How did God make up to Job the loss he suffered? _____

_____

EXODUS

NAME: Exodus means "going out." Exodus tells of the going out of the children of Israel from Egypt.

AUTHOR: Moses.

DATE: About 1500 BC

KEY TEXT: "Then they cried unto the Lord in their trouble, and he saved them out of their distresses" Psalm 107:13.

OUTLINE: *(Learn)*

    I.   Israel delivered from Egypt (Ex. 1–18)
        A.   Bondage and deliverer
        B.   Contest and deliverance
        C.   From the Red Sea to Sinai

    II. Israel at Mt. Sinai (Ex. 19–40)
        A.   Law given
        B.   Tabernacle and worship plans given
        C.   Law broken
        D.   Tabernacle made and set up.

ISRAEL DELIVERED FROM EGYPT—(EXODUS 1–18)

BONDAGE AND DELIVERER (1–4)

1.   Why did Pharaoh of Egypt make the Israelites his slaves? (1:9–10)_____
_____

2.   In what ways did he oppress them?_____
_____

3.   *Exodus 1 covers about 350 years. Contrast the numbers, situation, and treatment of the Israelites at the beginning and the end of this chapter:*

Beginning	End
_____	_____
_____	_____
_____	_____

4.   Moses was chosen by God as Israel's **deliverer**. How are the following people related to him?
     Amram (6:20) _____   Aaron _____
     Jochebed (6:20)_____   Zipporah_____
     Miriam _____   Jethro _____

5.   What did Moses learn in each of the following places which prepared him for his life's work? *(Read Acts 7:22–30 also)*
    a.   In his mother's home_____
       _____

    b.   In Pharaoh's palace_____
       _____

    c.   In the wilderness of Midian_____
       _____

6.   Why was Moses' opportunity for education greater than others of his day? _____
_____

7. What great decision was made by Moses at 40 years of age? (See Hebrews 11:25–28) _____
    _____
    _____

8. How old was Moses when he went into the wilderness? (Acts 7:23–30) _____
    How old was he when he returned to Egypt? _____
    How old was he when he died? (Deuteronomy 34:7) _____

9. *Be able to describe Moses' call. When, where and how. List Moses' excuses and God's answers:*
    a. Moses said (3:11) _____
        God answered_____
    b. Moses said (4:1) _____
        God answered by giving him three signs:
        1. _____
        2. _____
        3. _____
    c. Moses said (4:10) _____
        God answered _____

10. Who joined Moses as his spokesman? _____

11. To whom did they first bring their message of deliverance? (4:29–31)_____

CONTEST AND DELIVERANCE (5–13)

1. What did Moses and Aaron ask Pharaoh? (5)_____
    _____

2. What were the results? _____
    _____

3. Pharaoh said, "Who is the LORD, that I should obey his voice to let Israel go?" What did God do to
    answer this question?_____
    _____
    _____

4. For what other reasons did God send the ten plagues?_____
    _____
    _____

5. The ten plagues were: (7–12)   Associated with:
    1. _____ }
    2. _____ } River
    3. _____ }
    4. _____ } Insects
    5. _____ }
    6. _____ } Disease
    7. _____ }
    8. _____ } Crops
    9. _____ }
    10. _____ } Severity

6. Which plagues did the magicians attempt to duplicate?_____
    _____

7. Which plagues did not affect the Israelites? (List the numbers) _____
   _____

8. What shows that the plagues did not happen by chance? _____
   _____

9. When the plagues came what did Pharaoh say?_____
   _____

10. When the plagues left what did he do?_____

11. What two things did the Israelites do with the lamb? (12:3–8) _____
    _____
    _____

12. On what three places was the blood put?_____
    _____

13. What happened at midnight in the homes of the Egyptians? _____
    _____

14. Why was the feast called the Passover?_____
    _____

    (The **Passover** became one of the most important religious festivals of the Israelites and is observed
    even now by many Jews.)

15. *Describe what you believe were the Israelites' thoughts and feelings during the evening.*
    _____
    _____
    _____

16. Why was the Passover feast to be kept in the years to come? (12:14–20) _____
    _____

17. Who is our Passover Lamb whose blood protects us from the judgment of God? (1 Corinthians 5:7)
    _____

18. What did Pharaoh and the Egyptians tell the Israelites that night? (12:29–36)_____
    _____

19. As they left what did the Israelites take from the Egyptians? _____

20. How many Israelite men left Egypt?_____
    *(Counting women and children there were probably over two million Israelites who came out of Egypt with
    Moses.)*

21. Why did God lead Israel the long way through the wilderness to Canaan? (13:17–18)_____
    _____
    _____

22. How did God lead Israel in the way? (13:21–22)_____
    _____

FROM THE RED SEA TO SINAI (14–18)

1. What did God promise the Israelites in Exodus 6:1–9? _____
   _____
   _____
   _____

2. How did God deliver Israel completely at the Red Sea? (14)_____

_____

_____

_____

_____

3. How did Israel express her gratitude and praise to God? (15)_____

_____

4. *Underline in your Bible the names and descriptions of God in Exodus 15:1–18.*

5. *Name a Christian hymn that expresses one's gratitude for God's deliverance and help.*

_____

6. *List what happened at each stop:*
   a. Rameses (12:37)—starting place
   b. Succoth (12:37, 13:20)—first stop
   c. Red Sea (14–15)_____

   _____

   d. Marah (15:23–26)_____

   _____

   e. Elim (15:27)_____

   _____

   f. Wilderness of Sin (16)_____

   _____

   _____

   g. Rephidim (17–18)
      1. (17:1–7) _____

      _____

      2. (17:8–16)_____

      _____

      3. (18)_____

      _____

7. *Trace the journey on the map, page 29.* Have you completed this?_____

ISRAEL AT MT. SINAI—EXODUS 19–40

LAW GIVEN (19–24)

1. How did the people prepare to meet with God? (19) _____

_____

_____

2. How were the ten commandments (Israel's Constitution) first given? (20:1)_____

_____

3. *Memorize the TEN COMMANDMENTS in their short form: (20:3–17)*

   I. Thou shalt have no other gods before me.

   What are some of the things people put before God today?_____

   _____

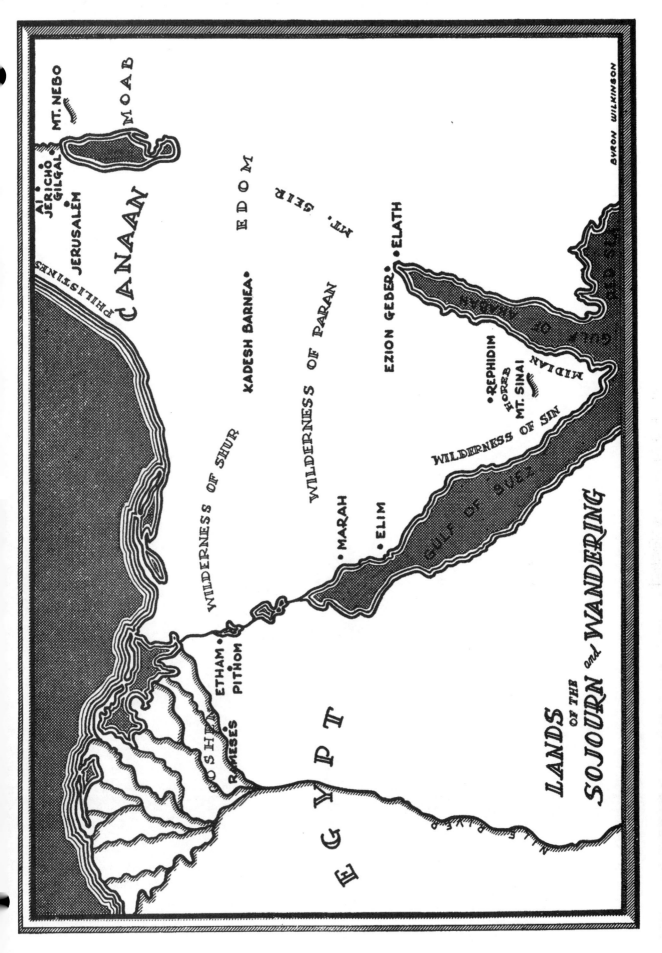

LANDS of the SOJOURN and WANDERING

BYRON WILKINSON

II. Thou shalt not make unto thee any graven image.

Why does God not want men to make images? _____

_____

III. Thou shalt not take the name of the Lord thy God in vain.

How does one show respect for God's name? _____

_____

_____

IV. Remember the sabbath day to keep it holy.

What does the Bible teach about what we do on the sabbath day? (34:21, Isa. 58:13–14, Luke

4:16, Matt. 12:12, Mark 2:27–28) _____

_____

_____

_____

_____

V. Honor thy father and thy mother.

How does one honor his parents? _____

_____

VI. Thou shalt not kill.

What common attitudes are a breaking of the command not to kill? (Matt. 5:21–22)_____

_____

VII. Thou shalt not commit adultery.

How does Jesus further explain the command about adultery? (Matt. 5:27–28, 31–32) _____

_____

_____

VIII. Thou shalt not steal.

In what ways are respected people often tempted to break this? _____

_____

_____

_____

IV. Thou shalt not bear false witness.

What causes people to break this command?_____

_____

X. Thou shalt not covet.

Why is coveting as bad or like idolatry? (See Col. 3:5b)_____

_____

4. The Old Testament laws of Moses included:
   a. **Moral law**   Rules of right and wrong   Ten commandments
   b. **Civil law**   Rules for the nation
   c. **Ceremonial laws** Rules of worship   In Leviticus

TABERNACLE AND WORSHIP PLANS GIVEN (25–31)

LAW BROKEN (32–34)

1. How did the people sin? (32)_____

2. What was the result of Moses' prayer for the people? _____

_____

3. *List all the ways you can find in which the people were punished.* _____

_____

_____

_____

TABERNACLE MADE AND SET UP (35–40)

(Making a model to scale of the tabernacle and its furnishings is most instructive and enjoyable.)

1. Be able to discuss each of the following:
   a. The name, "tabernacle"
   b. Purpose
   c. Financing
   d. Builders
   e. Materials used
   f. Shape
   g. Size (1 cu. = 1½ ft.)
   h. Furniture

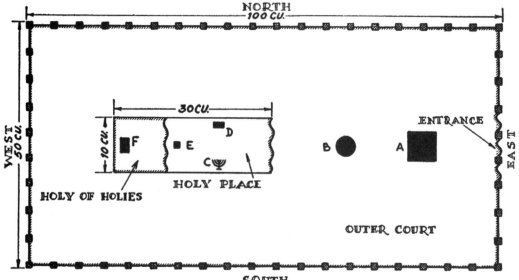

2. *Name the articles of furniture in the above diagram:*

   A. _____   D. _____

   B. _____   E. _____

   C. _____   F. _____

3. *Place the letter of the piece of furniture which best seems to picture the following:*

   _____ Christ, the sacrifice for sin   _____ Christ, the bread of life

   _____ Christ, the cleanser from sin   _____ Prayer, in Jesus' name

   _____ Christ, the light of the world   _____ God's dwelling place

LEVITICUS

Read Leviticus 10:1–7, 11:1–8, 16, 23, 25:1–17

NAME: Leviticus comes from Levi, the name of the priestly tribe. It is a handbook for the priests and worshipers.

AUTHOR: Moses, in 1500 BC at Mt. Sinai.

OUTLINE:
- A. The way to God (Leviticus 1–16)
- B. The walk with God (Leviticus 17–27)

THEME: Holiness in worship and walk.

The key word is "holy."

THE WAY TO GOD MUST BE ACCORDING TO GOD'S COMMAND
1. Who tried to come to God their own way? (10:1) _____
2. What was their punishment? _____

THE WAY TO GOD WAS THROUGH SACRIFICES
Of the five types of sacrifices the **burnt offering, meal offering,** and **peace offering** were called sweet-savor offerings and were especially for worship.

The **sin offering** and the **trespass offering** were especially for pardon.

1. Through whose sacrifice do we have a way to God? (See Heb. 9:25–26, Heb. 10:14, John 14:6)

    _____

2. What were two characteristics that would make an animal a clean animal—suitable for sacrifice and for eating? (11:1–3) _____

    _____

3. What animals are of this kind? _____

    _____

4. Name five unclean animals not to be eaten. *(Glance over the animals mentioned in Lev. 11)*

    _____

    _____

THE WAY TO GOD WAS SOUGHT ON THE DAY OF ATONEMENT

Leviticus 16 is the great salvation and Christ-picturing chapter in Leviticus such as Genesis 22 and Exodus 12 were in these books.

1. **The day of Atonement,** a fast day, not a feast day, was kept once a year.
2. The people stopped work and with a deep sense of sin sought God's forgiveness.
3. Once a year on the day of Atonement the high priest alone went into the Holy of Holies.
    - A. Laying aside his priestly robes he dressed in plain garments.
    - B. Taking incense and the _____ from a slain bullock, he entered the Holy of Holies, sprinkled the _____ seat _____ times, making atonement for himself and his family.
    - C. Entering the Holy of Holies again and with the blood of a _____ he sprinkled the _____ seat, making atonement for the sins of the people.
    - D. Having laid hands on the head of another _____ and confessed the nation's _____ he sent this scapegoat into the _____ from which it never returned. *(Read Ps. 103:12)*

    In what ways is Christ like this high priest? (Heb. 9:12, 24)

    _____

    _____

THE WALK WITH GOD INCLUDED THE CELEBRATION OF SEVEN WONDERFUL FEASTS:

Leviticus 23 describes these seven **feasts.**

1. PASSOVER
2. Unleavened Bread
3. First Fruits   Centered around Passover in the spring
4. PENTECOST
5. Trumpets
6. Atonement (a fast day)   Centered around Atonement in the fall
7. TABERNACLES

At the feasts of Passover, Pentecost, and Tabernacles all the adult males were supposed to attend.

Some purposes of these feasts were:

1. They united the nation.
2. They provided joyous rest and recreation.
3. They were means of a devout worship of God.
4. They celebrated the past goodness of God.

THE WALK WITH GOD INCLUDED HAVING THE SABBATIC YEAR AND THE YEAR OF JUBILEE

1. What did God command to be done every seventh year? (25:4–6) _____
_____

2. What did God command to be done every fiftieth year? (25:10–17) _____
_____

NUMBERS

Read Numbers 12, 14, 16, 17, 20 and suggested references

NAME: Called Numbers because it tells of two numberings of the Israelites. The Hebrew title "In the Wilderness" is better.

AUTHOR: Moses, in about 1500 BC

TIME COVERED: 39 years of wandering.

1. When the Israelites were numbered how many men above twenty years of age were counted? (1:2–3; 2:32) _____

   (If you added women and children there were probably two million and a half or three million Israelites.)

2. *Memorize the benediction in Numbers 6:24–26.*

3. Why did Miriam and Aaron murmur against Moses? (12) _____
   _____

4. How did God show his disapproval of them? _____
   _____

5. Who prayed for Miriam's healing? _____

6. How many men were sent to spy out Canaan? (13:2) _____

7. Tell the things the spies reported about Canaan. (13:23–33)
   a. Good _____
   b. Bad _____

8. What two spies believed Israel could capture Canaan? (14:6–9) _____
   _____

9. Did the Israelites believe God could give them the land? _____

10. What punishment did God consider? (14:12) _____
    _____

11. How did Moses reason against this? (14:13–16) _____
    _____

12. How did God punish Israel's unbelief? _____
    _____

13. Upon hearing of their punishment, what did the Israelites suddenly decide to do? _____
    _____

14. How did Korab, Dathan, and Abram sin? (16) _____
    _____

15. What was their unusual punishment? _____

16. What did God do to show the people He had chosen Aaron and the Levites for priests? (17)
    _____
    _____

17. What did God tell Moses to do to provide water for the murmuring Israelites? (20)
    _____

18. What did Moses do? _____

19. What was Moses' punishment for this sin? _____
    _____

20. Why did the Israelites have to go around the land of Edom? _____
    _____

21. When Aaron died at Mt. Hor, who became the next high priest? _____

22. When they murmured again how were the Israelites punished? (21:5–9) _____
    _____

23. How were they healed? _____
    _____

24. In what way is this similar to our being healed from the deadly bite of sin? (John 3:14–15)
    _____
    _____

25. Who won in Israel's battle against Sihon, king of the Amorites? (21:21–25) _____

26. Who won when Israel battled Og, king of Bashan? (21:33–35) _____
    (Students may be assigned to tell the story of Balaam and Balak found in Numbers 22–24 and in Bible story books.)

27. *Read the prophecy of Christ in Numbers 24:17.*

28. Whom did Moses appoint as his successor? (27:18–20) _____

29. Who won in Israel's battle against Midian? (31:1–8) _____

30. Which tribes asked to stay on the east side of Jordan? (32:1, 5) _____

31. *Read the instructions for possessing Canaan. (33:51–56)*

32. *On the map, page 29, trace Israel's journey from Sinai to Kadesh-Bamea, the 38 years' wandering, back to Kadesh-Barnea, then to the south of Edom and Mt. Sier up to the east side of Jordan. Put a check here when your map work is completed.* _____

DEUTERONOMY

Read Deuteronomy 6, 31 :1–13, 32:48–52, 34

NAME: "Deuteronomy" means "second law." Moses in this great farewell address needed to repeat the law to the new generation of Israelites.

KEY NOTE: Obedience.

SCENE: In the Plains of Moab, east of Jordan.

TIME: At the close of the 40 years wandering, just before the people were to enter Canaan.

AUTHOR: Moses gave the orations of this book orally and then wrote them. (Read 1:3 and 31:24–26) Deuteronomy 34 was probably added by Joshua.

MESSAGE: Moses reviewed the past in order to emphasize the gratitude, obedience, and loyalty that the people should show to God in the future. Jesus quoted three times from Deuteronomy in resisting Satan's temptations.

THINGS FOR YOU TO DO:

Notice and mark the many precious promises in the book as you read.

1. Deuteronomy 6
   Underline five verses that you consider excellent commands and instructions for our day as well as their time.

2. Deuteronomy 31:1–13
   Place yourself among the Israelites hearing these words of Moses. How do you imagine that you would have felt about conquering Canaan?

   _____

   _____

   This book was to be read publicly every _____ years at the feast of _____.

3. Deuteronomy 32:48–52
   God told _____ to go to Mount _____ in the land of _____ and _____ in the mountain because he had not sanctified God in the midst of the children of Israel.

4. Deuteronomy 34
   Moses was _____ years old when he died; his eye was not _____ nor his natural_____ abated. There arose not a _____ since in Israel like unto _____ whom the Lord knew face to face.

   List six things that you admire about Moses. _____

   _____

   _____

   _____

   _____

JOSHUA

BOOK OF VICTORY

Read Joshua 1–3, 5:11–11:23, 23, 24

THEME: Conquest and division of the Promised Land

TIME COVERED: About 30 years. Joshua was 80 years old when he took command and 110 at his death. He was about 7 years subduing the land and the 23 remaining years were occupied in settling and establishing the tribes.

OUTLINE OF JOSHUA: *(Learn the A. B. C. divisions.)* As you read, fill in the following outline of the book:

CONQUEST OF CANAAN (1–12)

I. **JOSHUA, THE LEADER**

    a. His preparation for the work

        1. As a military general leading the forces of Israel at Rephidim.

        2. As Moses' minister. Was with Moses in the mount.

        3. Had seen God's miracles in Egypt and on the journey.

        4. As one of the twelve spies to enter Canaan.

        5. Had the Spirit of God.

    b. God's promises to him (1:3, 5, 9). *Underline these in your Bible.*

    c. Joshua's command to the people (1:10–11) _____

    _____

    d. The people's response to Joshua (1:16–17) _____

    _____

II. **THE WORK OF THE TWO SPIES (2)**

    a. Rahab's attitude toward Israel and the cause (2:11)_____

    _____

    b. The attitude of the people of Canaan (2:24)_____

III. **CENTRAL CANAAN TAKEN**

    a. The Jordan crossed (3) *(Locate the Jordan River on the map, page 39)*

        1. People's preparation_____

        _____

        2. Miracles performed _____

        _____

        3. Order of march _____

        _____

        4. Memorials set up. Twelve stones were taken from the middle of the river and placed in Gilgal as a memorial to God's dividing the water. Joshua also placed another similar monument in the midst of the river where the priests had stood with the ark.

        5. Effect on the Canaanites (5) _____

        _____

        6. The Passover was kept at Gilgal *(Locate on the map.)*

        7. New food (5:11)_____

        8. The unseen Captain (5:13–15) _____

        _____

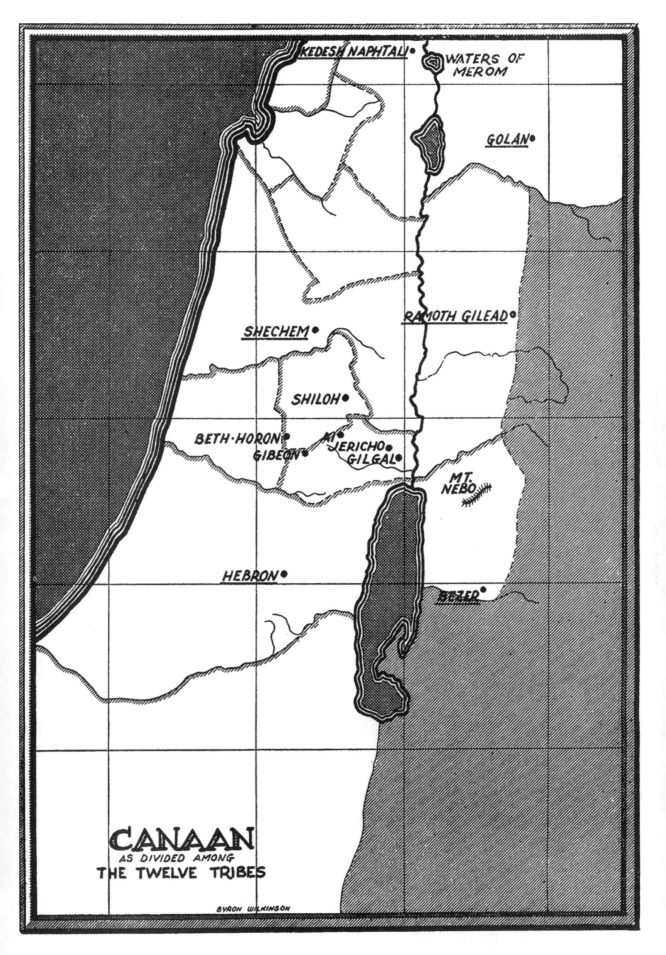

KEDESH NAPHTALI •
WATERS OF MEROM
GOLAN •
RAMOTH GILEAD •
SHECHEM •
SHILOH •
BETH·HORON •
AI •
GIBEON •
JERICHO •
GILGAL •
MT. NEBO
HEBRON •
BEZER •

CANAAN
AS DIVIDED AMONG
THE TWELVE TRIBES

BYRON WILKINSON

    b. The conquest of Jericho (6) *(Locate on the map.)*

        1. Method of attack _____

_____

_____

_____

        2. Restrictions placed upon the people _____

_____

        3. Result _____

        4. Curse pronounced (6:26) _____

_____

    c. The conquest of Ai (7–8) *(Locate on the map.)*

        1. Cause of failure _____

_____

        2. Sin confessed and punished _____

_____

        3. Victory _____

_____

    d. League with the Gibeonites (9) *(Locate on the map.)*

        1. God's command recalled (Deut. 7:1–2) _____

_____

        2. Trick of the Gibeonites _____

_____

        3. Cause of Joshua's being deceived (9:14) _____

_____

        4. Result _____

_____

IV. CONQUEST OF SOUTHERN CANAAN—BATTLE WITH THE FIVE KINGS (10)

    a. Joshua's surprise attack _____

_____

    b. God's help at Beth-Horon *(Locate on the map.)*

_____

    c. Miraculous phenomena connected with the victory _____

_____

    d. Cause of the victory _____

_____

V. CONQUEST OF NORTHERN CANAAN (11)

    a. Scene of battle (11:5) *(Locate on the map.)*

_____

    b. Result _____

_____

    c. *Have you located on the map all the places mentioned above?*

CANAAN DIVIDED AMONG THE TRIBES (13–21)

Locate and write in the names of these tribes on the map. Note especially the location of Judah and Ephraim.

I. Each tribe was given a portion of the land according to the number in the tribe.

II. Caleb requested territory around Hebron *(locate on map)*, including the Cave of Machpelah where Abraham, Isaac, Jacob, and their wives were buried.

III. Tabernacle was set up at Shiloh (18:1) *(Locate on the map.)*

IV. Tribes east of the Jordan returned after helping the others conquer the land west of Jordan.

V. Six cities of refuge for innocent killers were appointed. *(See underlined names, page 39.)*

VI. The Levites were given as their portion 48 cities scattered throughout Canaan. These included the six cities of refuge.

JOSHUA'S LAST COUNSEL AND DEATH (23–24)

I. To whom was Joshua's last counsel given?_____

II. Instructions (23) *Mark the portions that impress you.*

III. God's promises recalled (24)_____

_____

_____

IV. Challenge given (24:14)_____

V. Joshua's decision (24:15)_____

_____

VI. Warnings given (23:12–13; 24:20) _____

_____

VII. Promise of the people _____

_____

VIII. His burial, age, and tribe _____

_____

IX. Joseph's bones_____

_____

X. What qualities made Joshua such an outstanding leader? _____

_____   _____   _____

_____   _____   _____

JUDGES
BOOK OF DEFEAT

Read Judges 3, 4, 6, 7, 11, 13–16

AUTHOR: Unknown. Tradition says Samuel.

TIME COVERED: Probably 200 to 300 years. Known as the "Dark Ages" of Israel's history.

KEY VERSE: Judges 21:25—"In those days there was no king in Israel: every man did that which was right in his own eyes."

OUTLINE OF GOD'S REPEATED DEALINGS WITH ISRAEL:

1. Sin—Israel fell into sin and idolatry.
2. Punishment—God let their enemies overrun them.
3. Repentance—They cried unto the Lord.
4. Deliverance—The Lord raised up a judge to deliver them.
    (Study Judges 2:11–19 as a brief summary or sample of the entire book.)

EVENTS: Seven times the above cycle occurs:

	Scripture	Conqueror	Length	Judge	Time of rest
1.	3:1–11	**King of Mesopotamia**	8 years	**Othniel**	40 years
2.	3:12–31	**Eglon, king of Moab,** and the Philistines	18 years	**Ehud,** Shamgar	80 years
3.	4–5	**Jabin, king of Canaan**	20 years	**Deborah, Barak**	40 years
4.	6–8:32	**Midianites**	7 years	**Gideon**	40 years
5.	8:33–10:5	Civil war, etc.	unknown	Abimelech, Tola, Jair	
6.	10:6–12:15	Ammonites	18 years	**Jephthah,** Ibzan, Elon, Abdon	
7.	13–16	**Philistines**	40 years	**Samson**	20 years

(Notice Hebrews 11:32)

THINGS FOR YOU TO DO:

1. *Be able to tell interestingly and completely the story of each important judge.*

2. *Write an article for the newspaper about Barak and Deborah, Gideon, Jephthah, or Samson. Make it either a NEWS ARTICLE, giving the main facts of the hero, what he or she did and why, or a FEATURE ARTICLE, giving an eyewitness account of the battle or other events, or an EDITORIAL, giving the character of the judge, his or her faithfulness to God, etc. Newspaper articles must be accurate, you know.*

3. *Match the following statements with the name of some judge:*

    1. _____ son-in-law of Caleb
    2. _____ left-handed
    3. _____ prophetess
    4. _____ destroyed father's idol, Baal
    5. _____ foolish vow
    6. _____ loved Delilah
    7. _____ fleece

8. _____ long hair
9. _____ defeated Midian with 300 men
10. _____ inspired by Deborah to fight Canaanites
11. _____ destroyed temple of Dagon
12. _____ daughter met him after the victory
13. _____ slew 600 Philistines with an ox goad
14. _____ a Nazarite
15. _____ pitchers and torches
16. _____ made blind
17. _____ assassinated King Eglon of Moab
18. _____ killed more in his death than in his life
19. _____ called by angel while threshing wheat
20. _____ birth was announced to his mother and father

RUTH

Read Ruth 1–4

DATE: "In the days when the judges ruled." (Ruth 1:1)

AUTHOR: Tradition says that Samuel wrote both Judges and Ruth. At one time Ruth was a part of the book of Judges.

OUTLINE:

Chapter 1	Ruth's choice	Naomi plans to return home.
Chapter 2	Ruth's service	Ruth's plan to make a living.
Chapter 3	Ruth's romance	Naomi's plan for Ruth's marriage.
Chapter 4	Ruth's reward	Boaz's plans.

OLD CUSTOMS:

1. A widow should marry her husband's nearest relative. (Deut. 25:5–9)
2. The poor had the privilege of gleaning (picking up the grain) behind the reapers.
3. A widow would lie down at the feet of her husband's relative to indicate her willingness to marry him.
4. The kinsman's shoe was relinquished as a sign of giving up his right to the widow and property of the relative who had died.

THINGS FOR YOU TO DO:

1. *Be able to identify Elimelech, Naomi, Mahlon, Chilion, Orpah, Ruth, and Boaz.*
2. *Locate Bethlehem, Judah, and Moab on the map, page 39.*
3. *Memorize Ruth 1:16–17.*
4. *Complete the following story:*

THE STORY OF RUTH:

_____ and _____ and their two sons, _____ and _____, left _____ because there was a _____ in the land. They came to the country of _____. Elimelech _____ in Moab. There the sons married _____ and _____ and later the sons also _____. Then Naomi decided to go back to the land of_____. _____ stayed with her people in Moab but _____ went with her mother-in-law, _____, back to the town of _____. Because of her bitter experience in Moab, Naomi told her old friends to call her _____. _____ showed her love and her helpfulness by going to _____ in the barley fields of a _____ man named _____. He was kind to _____ and she gleaned in his field till the end of the harvest. The _____ kinsman could not _____ Ruth so he took off his _____ and gave it to Boaz. _____ and _____ were married. Later they became the great-grandparents of Israel's greatest king, _____.

What is the connection of this story with Jesus? (Matt. 1:5, Ruth 1:19, and Luke 2:8, 15)

_____

_____

What do you admire about Ruth? _____

_____

_____

What do you admire about Boaz? _____

_____

_____

What part did God have in the story? _____

_____

_____

THE UNITED AND DIVIDED KINGDOM
Contents of Historical Books of the Kingdom

1 Samuel: Samuel, reign of Saul, early life of David

2 Samuel: Reign of David

1 Kings: Solomon and the divided kingdoms

2 Kings: The divided kingdoms and their fall

1 Chronicles covers nearly the same period as 2 Samuel (David).

2 Chronicles covers nearly the same period as 1 and 2 Kings (Solomon and other kings after him).

1 and 2 Chronicles differ from 2 Samuel and 1 and 2 Kings in that more emphasis is placed on the Southern Kingdom, the temple, the priests, and the divine interpretation or philosophy of the history.

THE UNITED KINGDOM

How many can you identify clearly now? Try again later:

1. Eli _____
2. Elkanah _____
3. Hannah _____
4. Samuel _____
5. Saul _____
6. Jesse _____
7. David _____
8. Goliath _____
9. Jonathan _____
10. Michal _____
11. Abner _____
12. Joab _____
13. Mephibosheth _____
14. Uriah _____
15. Bathsheba _____
16. Solomon_____
17. Absalom _____
18. Nathan _____
19. Queen of Sheba _____
20. Hiram _____

PREPARATIONS FOR THE KINGDOM—SAMUEL (1 SAMUEL 1–3, 7)

I. Samuel's position—the last of the judges and the anointer of kings.

   a. Prophet: the first of a long line of writing prophets.

     A "prophet" is _____

     _____

   b. Priest

     A "priest" is_____

     _____

   c. Judge: the last of the line of judges. He delivered Israel from the Philistines by prayer. Israel's government until the time of Saul and the kings was a theocracy. ("Theocracy" means a government with God as king.)

II. Samuel's mother (1:1–2:11)
    a. Why was she sorrowful?_____
    b. What did she pray for?_____
    c. What did she vow? _____
    d. Her song was like whose? (Luke 1:46–55) _____

III. Samuel's childhood (2:11–3:21)
    a. What evil influences surrounded him? _____
    _____
    b. What good influences were in his life?_____
    _____
    c. What contact did he have with his mother?_____
    _____
    d. What reproof and warning did God give Eli? _____
    _____
    _____
    _____
    e. How many times did God call Samuel?_____
    f. What did God tell Samuel? _____
    _____
    _____
    _____

IV. Samuel as judge (7)
    a. What was Samuel's plea? (7:3–4)_____
    _____
    b. What did the people request of Samuel at the time of trouble with the Philistines? (7:7–9)
    _____
    c. What three offices or kinds of work did Samuel perform? (9:9)_____
    (7:9) _____   (7:15) _____

THE FIRST KING—SAUL (1 SAMUEL 8–10; 12; 13:1–14; 15)

I. The people's request for a king (8)
    a. Why? _____
    _____
    b. What was the effect on Samuel?_____
    _____
    c. What did God say about this request?_____
    _____
    d. What burdens would a king place upon their
    sons_____
    daughters _____
    possessions_____

II. Saul chosen as king (9–10)
    a. His father's name? _____

b. From what tribe? _____

c. Describe Saul's appearance: _____
_____

d. How and where was he first anointed? _____
_____
_____

e. What predictions did Samuel make? (10:2–8)_____
_____
_____
_____
_____

f. Where was Saul publicly selected?_____

g. What quality of disposition did Saul show? _____

h. How did the people receive their new king? _____
_____

i. What city did Saul first help? (11:1–11) _____

III. Samuel's farewell address (12)

a. To what temptations as a ruler did Samuel never yield? _____
_____
_____

a. What did the people request and Samuel promise? (12:19, 23)_____
_____

IV. Saul's rejection (13:1–14; 15)

a. Why did Saul assume the authority of a priest and offer a sacrifice? ____
_____

b. What was the result? (13:13–14)_____
_____

c. How did Saul disobey God in regard to the Amalekites? (15:1–9)_____
_____
_____

d. What was God's attitude? (15:22, 23) _____
_____
_____

SAUL AND DAVID (1 SAMUEL 16–18; 20; 24; 26; 28; 31)

I. David's youth (16–17)

a. His father?_____

b. His tribe?_____

c. His birthplace?_____

d. His occupation and skills?_____
_____

e. His appearance? _____

f. Who anointed him to be the second king?_____

g. When did David first meet Saul?_____
_____

h. How did David happen to see Goliath? _____

_____

i. Why did David resent Goliath's challenge? _____

_____

j. Why did David refuse to use Saul's armor? _____

_____

k. *List everything in David's training and experience that prepared him for his victory over Goliath.*

_____

_____

II. Saul's jealousy of David (18)

a. Why? _____

_____

b. What ways did he try to kill David? (18:11, 13, 17, 20–25; 19:10–17) _____

_____

_____

_____

III. Jonathan, Saul's son

a. With whom did he make a love covenant? (18:1–3) _____

b. How did Jonathan warn David of danger? (20) _____

_____

_____

IV. David an outlaw from Saul (24, 26)

a. Where and how did David first spare Saul's life? _____

_____

_____

b. What great national leader died? (25:1) _____

c. Where did David spare Saul's life the second time? _____

_____

d. Why was Abner rebuked? _____

_____

V. End of Saul's reign (28, 31)

a. Why did Saul visit the witch of Endor? _____

_____

b. What were the results of the Philistine battle? _____

_____

THE SECOND KING—DAVID (2 SAMUEL 2:1–12; 5–7; 11; 12; 15:1–18; 18)

1. **His shepherd life** ⎫
2. **His court life**   ⎬ **1 Samuel**
3. **His outlaw life**   ⎭
4. **His royal life at Hebron**   ⎫ **2 Samuel**
5. **His royal life at Jerusalem** ⎭

I.   David, king over Judah (2:1–12)

    a.   What was David's attitude toward the men of Jabesh-Gilead who had buried Saul?

       _____

    b.   Who was king over the eleven tribes?_____

    c.   How long did David rule in Hebron over Judah? (2:1, 11)_____

II.   David, king over all Israel (5)

    a.   His age? _____

    b.   Length of his reigns?_____

    c.   What city was captured for the capital? _____

       (Look up its early history in a reference material.)

III.   David's experiences with the ark of the covenant (6)

    a.   Why was David's good intention a failure?_____

IV.   David's great desire to build a temple (7)

    a.   Why was it not granted? _____

    b.   What did God promise David? (7:12–16) _____

       _____

       _____

    c.   What is David's place in God's plan of redemption? (7:16, Luke 1:32)_____

V.   David's kindness to Saul's house (9)

    a.   How shown?_____

       _____

VI.   David's sin (11–12)

    a.   When did David sin?_____

    b.   What method was used to bring David to repentance? _____

       _____

    c.   What does Psalm 51 show of David's heart experience? _____

       _____

       _____

    d.   Who was Bathsheba's next son? _____

VII.   David's trouble with his sons—Absalom and Adonijah

    a.   How did Absalom win the hearts of the people? (15:1–18)_____

       _____

       _____

    b.   Who led the exiled David's forces in battle?_____

    c.   What was David's attitude toward the news of his rebellious son's death?_____

       _____

       _____

    d.   What did David's son Adonijah plan? (1 Kings 1:5) _____

       _____

VIII.   David's charge to Solomon and his death *(See Solomon)*

    STUDY the writings of David, pages 55–56.

THE THIRD KING—SOLOMON (1 KINGS 2:1–12; 3; 6; 8; 10; 11)

I. David's charge to Solomon (2:1–4)

    a. What did he urge Solomon to do? _____

    _____

    _____

II. Solomon's wisdom (3)

    a. When and why did he receive wisdom? _____

    _____

    _____

    b. What court decision demonstrated his wisdom? _____

    _____

    _____

III. Solomon's temple (5, 6, 8)

    a. What did he request of Hiram, king of Tyre? _____

    _____

    b. *Read about Solomon's temple in a reference material.*

    c. How long did the building take? (6:1, 38) _____

    d. In Solomon's message and prayer underline all the words that would be appropriate to a nation or a church today.

    e. *Memorize 2 Chron. 7:14–15*

IV. Solomon's splendor (10, 11)

    a. Who visited Solomon and what impression did she receive? _____

    _____

    _____

    b. *Describe Solomon's throne.* _____

    _____

    _____

    c. What kind of trade did Solomon have? _____

    _____

    _____

V. Solomon's failure (11)

    a. What influence did Solomon's wives have on him? _____

    _____

    b. What was God's message to Solomon? (11:9–13) _____

    _____

    _____

STUDY the writings of Solomon, pages 56–58.

QUOTATIONS FROM THE UNITED KINGDOM PERIOD

In front of each of the following quotations place the name of one of the following who spoke the words:

God	Saul	Nathan
The people	David	Absalom
Samuel	Solomon	Queen of Sheba

After the quotation write "to whom" or "when" it was said.

1. _____ said "Speak, Lord, for thy servant heareth." _____
_____

2. _____ said "Give us a king to judge us." _____
_____

3. _____ said "God save the king." _____
_____

4. _____ said "Because I saw the people were scattered from me, and that thou camest not. . . . I forced myself therefore, and offered a burnt offering."
_____

5. _____ said "Behold to obey is better than sacrifice, and to harken than the fat of rams." _____

6. _____ said "For thou hast rejected the word of the Lord, and the Lord hath rejected thee from being king over Israel." _____
_____

7. _____ said "For man looketh on the outward appearance, but the Lord looketh on the heart." _____
_____

8. _____ said "Thou comest to me with a sword, and with a spear, and with a shield; but I come to thee in the name of the Lord of hosts, the God of the armies of Israel, whom thou hast defied." _____
_____

9. _____ said "Saul has slain his thousands, and David his ten thousands."
_____

10. _____ said "The Lord forbid that I should stretch forth mine hand against the Lord's anointed." _____
_____

11. _____ said "Bring me up Samuel." _____
_____

12. _____ said "Draw thy sword, and thrust me through therewith." _____
_____

13. _____ said "See now, I dwell in an house of cedar, but the ark of God dwelleth within curtains." _____
_____

14. _____ said "Is there yet any that is left of the house of Saul, that I may show him kindness for Jonathan's sake?" _____
_____

15. _____ said "Thou art the man!" _____

_____

16. _____ said "Oh that I were made judge in the land, that every man which hath
any suit or cause might come unto me, and I would do him justice."

_____

17. _____ said "O my son Absalom, my son, my son Absalom!" _____

_____

18. _____ said "Ask what I shall give thee." _____

_____

19. _____ said "But will God indeed dwell on the earth? behold, the heaven and
heaven of heavens cannot contain thee; how much less this house that
I have builded?"_____

_____

20. _____ said "Behold, the half was not told me: thy wisdom and prosperity
exceedeth the fame which I heard."_____

_____

NATURE OF HEBREW POETRY

In Hebrew poetry the beauty rests not in the mechanical structure but in the thought. Its beauty is not lost in translation. The thing which makes Hebrew poetry is not word rhyme and rhythm but rather that which is called parallelism. Parallelism is "thought-rhythm" in "balanced lines." The American Standard Version Bible prints Hebrew poetry showing these lines.

KINDS OF PARALLELISM:

1. Synonymous—the second line repeats the meaning of the first in different words. Prov. 4:14, Ps. 103:10.

2. Synthetic—the second line does not repeat the first but adds a new thought to it. Prov. 16:25, 16:3, Eccl. 11:1.

3. Anthithetic—the second line is the opposite in meaning from the first. Prov. 14:34, 15:1.

PSALMS

"The inspired prayer and praise book of Israel"

PURPOSE: The Psalms are preeminently devotional. They were written to be sung. Worship is the central idea. Other parts of the Bible represent God speaking to man; here man is represented as speaking to God.

AUTHOR: David with 73 Psalms ascribed to him is the principal author though not the only one. Whose names are given with the following Psalms? 44_____, 72 _____, 73 _____, 90_____

TERMS: What do the following mean? *(Consult a Bible Dictionary or regular dictionary.)*

"Blessed" _____

"Hallelujah" _____

"Amen"_____

"Selah" _____

DIVISIONS: Into five books perhaps in imitation of the Pentateuch.

Book I	Psalms 1–41	Book IV	Psalms 90–106
Book II	Psalms 42–72	Book V	Psalms 107–150
Book III	Psalms 73–89		

Notice the close of each section.

MINOR COLLECTIONS within these books

1. Psalms of the Sons of Korah. (Psalms 44–49)
   The Sons of Korah were a family of poetic priests of David's time.

2. Psalms of Asaph. (Psalms 73–83)
   Asaph was one of David's choir leaders whose descendants led the songs for generations.

3. Theocratic Psalms. (Psalms 95–100). These praise the worth of Jehovah.

4. Hallel Psalms (Psalms 113–118)
   At the Passover Feast Psalms 113–114 were sung before the second cup; Psalms 115–118 after the fourth cup. This is probably the hymn Jesus and His disciples sang at the Last Supper. Mark 14:26.

5. Songs of "Ascents," or Song of "Degrees," or "Pilgrim Songs." (Psalms 120–134). These were designed to be sung by the people on their way up to the annual feasts at Jerusalem or as the priests mounted the steps to the temple court.

6. Hallelujah Psalms. (Psalms 146–150) *Notice the beginning and ending of each.*

TYPES OF PSALMS:

1. Psalms of instruction—1, 6, 7, 24, 82, 87, 119.
2. Psalms of praise and adoration—100, 107.
3. Psalms of thanksgiving—46, 48, 66, 68, 108.
4. Psalms of devotional prayers—6, 27, 61, 102, 120, 140, 141.
5. Historical Psalms—78, 105, 106.
6. Messianic Psalms—2, 16, 22, 40, 45, 72, 110.

    How do each of the following verses refer to Christ?

    Ps. 16:10 _____

    Ps. 22:7, 8 _____

    Ps. 22:16 _____

    Ps. 22:18 _____

    Ps. 31:5 _____

    Ps. 34:20 _____

    Ps. 41:9 _____

    Ps. 69:4 _____

    Ps. 69:21 _____

    Ps. 118:22 _____

7. Acrostic Psalms. The initial letters for each line or stanza of the poem are the twenty-two letters of the Hebrew alphabet in order. Ps. 25, 84, 119.

MORNING DEVOTIONS:

What does David say in Psalm 5:8? _____

_____

Do you already have a definite, daily, devotional time of prayer and praise? _____

If you do not, will you choose a time and meet God in prayer and Bible reading each day? This is vital and serious.

PROVERBS

"Laws from heaven for life on earth"

Proverbs is a book of practical ethics.

A proverb is a brief, wise saying regarding some practical or moral truth. It may have exceptions but is a general truth.

Solomon is the chief author of Proverbs as David is of Psalms.

How many proverbs did Solomon speak? (1 Kings 4:32) _____

THINGS TO DO:

Underline the most striking verses you read.

One profitable way to study proverbs is to think of Bible stories that illustrate the truth presented in each proverb.

Find out the teaching in Proverbs on the following practical everyday subjects:

1. Wrong companionship (1:10) _____

    _____

2. Guidance (8:5–6) _____

    _____

3. Wisdom (8:8–15) _____

    _____

4. Idleness (6:6–8) _____

_____

5. Things God hates (6:16–19) _____

_____

6. Duties of children to parent (6:20–21) _____

_____

7. Impurity (6:24–29) _____

_____

8. Honesty (11:1) _____

_____

9. Gossip (11:13) _____

_____

10. Liberality (11:24–25) _____

_____

11. Lying (12:22) _____

_____

12. Punishment (13:24) _____

_____

13. Work (14:23) _____

_____

14. National life (14:34) _____

_____

15. Courtesy (15:1) _____

_____

16. Humility (16:18) _____

_____

17. Self-control (16:32) _____

_____

18. True friendship (17:17; 18:24) _____

_____

19. Reputation (22:1) _____

_____

20. Drinking (23:29–32) _____

_____

21. Treatment of enemies (25:21–22) _____

_____

22. Meddling (26:17) _____

_____

23. Boasting (27:2) _____

_____

24. Contentment (30:8) _____

_____

25. The worthy woman (31:10–31) _____

_____

ECCLESIASTES

(This is a Greek word meaning "the preacher")

PROBLEM: How to find happiness in this life?

EXPERIMENT:

1. *List all the ways that Solomon tried to find happiness and satisfaction. (1:12–18); (2:1–15):*

   _____
   _____
   _____
   _____
   _____

2. Was Solomon in a position to get anything he desired?_____

3. *Notice the frequency with which "vanity" and "under the sun" occur.*
   What does "vanity" mean as used in Ecclesiastes? _____

   _____

   What does "under the sun" mean?_____

   _____

SOLUTION: Solomon's conclusion is found in Eccl. 12:13.

He found that there is no happiness apart from _____.

SONG OF SOLOMON

Solomon wrote a thousand and five songs (1 Kings 4:32) and this is called the "song of songs" because it is the best of them all.

It is a song of love in Oriental language, with rests, and pauses and varying scenery and conversation, sometimes considered as a "Wedding Day Drama" or a "Poem Celebrating a Royal Marriage."

The main speakers are a bride, called the "Shulamite," her lover, and a chorus of Jerusalem maidens.

Various meanings have been given to this love poem. One view is that it is an allegory. Under the figure of human love, the intimate, tender relationship existing between Christ and His people is set forth. The Jews read this book at the Passover as allegorically referring to the Exodus and Jehovah's love for Israel. In the New Testament the church is called the "bride" of Christ. Ephesians 5:28–32.

THE DIVIDED KINGDOM

THE DIVISION (READ 1 KINGS 11, 12)

1. What did Solomon do that caused God to permit the kingdom to divide? _____
   _____
   _____

2. How did the prophet Ahijah illustrate this coming division? _____

3. How was Rehoboam responsible for the split? _____
   _____
   _____

THE TWO KINGDOMS CONTRASTED

ISRAEL	JUDAH
Northern	Southern
Ten tribes	Two tribes
Capital first at Shechem then at Samaria	Capital at Jerusalem
Worshiped idols at Dan and Bethel	Worshiped at temple in Jerusalem
Nine different dynasties or families	One family
Nineteen kings	Nineteen kings, one queen
All bad kings	Good and bad kings
Shorter reigns	Longer reigns
Lasted about 240 years	Lasted 395 years
Kingdom fell in 722 BC	Kingdom fell in 587 BC
Taken into Assyria by Shalmanezer	Taken into Babylon by Nebuchadnezzar

```
                              Israel                    722 BC
   United Kingdom         ┌──────────────────────────────────
   ─────────────────      │                    To Assyria
   David—Solomon          │                                      587 BC
                          └──────────────────────────────────
                              Judah                     To Babylon
```

THE KINGS OF THE DIVIDED KINGDOMS

KINGS OF ISRAEL			KINGS OF JUDAH		
JEROBOAM	22 yrs.	Bad	REHOBOAM	17 yrs.	Bad
Nadab	2 yrs.	Bad	Abijah	3 yrs.	Bad
Baasha	24 yrs.	Bad	Asa	41 yrs.	Good
Elah	2 yrs.	Bad	Jehoshaphat	25 yrs.	Good
Zimri	7 days	Bad	Jehoram	8 yrs.	Bad
Omri	12 yrs.	Worse	Ahaziah	1 yr.	Bad
AHAB (Jezebel)	22 yrs.	The worst	(Athaliah)	6 yrs.	Terrible
Ahaziah	2 yrs.	Bad	Joash	40 yrs.	Fairly good
Jehoram	12 yrs.	Bad	Amaziah	29 yrs.	Fairly good
JEHU	28 yrs.	Bad	Uzziah	52 yrs.	Fairly good
Jehoahaz	17 yrs.	Bad	Jotham	16 yrs.	Fairly good
Joash	16 yrs.	Bad	Ahaz	16 yrs.	Wicked
Jeroboam II	41 yrs.	Bad	HEZEKIAH	29 yrs.	Very good
Zechariah	6 mo.	Bad	Manasseh	55 yrs.	Most wicked
Shallum	1 mo.	Bad	Amon	2 yrs.	Most wicked
Menahem	10 yrs.	Bad	JOSIAH	31 yrs.	Very good
Pekahiah	2 yrs.	Bad	Jehoahaz	3 mo.	Bad
Pekah	20 yrs.	Bad	Jehoikim	11 yrs.	Wicked
Hoshea	9 yrs.	Bad	Jehoiachin	3 yrs.	Bad
			Zedekiah	11 yrs.	Bad

STUDY FIRST THE KINGDOM OF ISRAEL: The above comparisons, the Prophets to Israel, page 61, and Israel's Captivity, page 63, *Read the chapters assigned.*

STUDY NEXT THE KINGDOM OF JUDAH: *In addition to studying the comparisons given, read and fill in the following:*

List all the activities of Hezekiah which prove he was truly a good king. (Read 2 Chronicles 29–32)

_____

_____

_____

_____

_____

_____

_____

List all the activities of Josiah which show him to be a good king, also. (Read 2 Chronicles 34–35)

_____

_____

_____

_____

_____

Study the Prophets of Judah, page 62 and the Captivity of Judah, page 63.

PROPHETS

The prophet was God's messenger bringing a message from God to men. The prophet and the priest both stand between God and man but the priest represents man and the prophet represents God.

Prophets not only told God's plan for the future but God's will for the present.

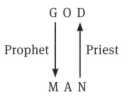

THE PROPHETS TO THE KINGDOM OF ISRAEL

(Listed in the probable order of their appearance)

ELIJAH *(Read 1 Kings 17, 18, 19, 2 Kings 2:1–12)*

List five story titles or five possible newspaper headlines for Elijah's life. Be able to tell each story vividly. Watch for the details.

1. _____
2. _____
3. _____
4. _____
5. _____

Notice particularly Elijah's first and last appearances.

ELISHA *(Read 1 Kings 19:19–21, 2 Kings 2; 5; 6; 7; 13:14–21)*

List the subjects for nine of Elisha's miracles. (Be able to tell each.)

1. 2 Kings 2:12 _____
2. 2 Kings 2:19 _____
3. 2 Kings 4:1 _____
4. 2 Kings 4:13 _____
5. 2 Kings 4:18 _____
6. 2 Kings 4:38 _____
7. 2 Kings 4:42 _____
8. 2 Kings 5:1 _____
9. 2 Kings 5:20 _____

JONAH *(Read Jonah 1–4)*

God commanded Jonah to go to _____. Instead of obeying he sailed from _____ in a boat going to_____. After a _____ arose the men cast Jonah into the _____. The Lord had _____ a great_____ which _____Jonah. After being_____ days inside the _____Jonah was cast out upon _____ _____. When God again commanded _____ to preach in _____ he went and preached saying "_____ _____ _____ _____ _____ _____ _____ _____." The people of Ninevah _____ _____.

When God did not bring destruction to the Gentile people of Ninevah Jonah felt _____ _____. Later when the sheltering gourd withered, Jonah felt _____.

God reproved Jonah saying, "_____ _____ _____." (4:10–11)

What do you think was the main reason Jonah had not wanted to preach in Nineveh in the first place? _____

_____

Read Romans 3:29 as a possible key text for the book of Jonah.
Read Matthew 12:40–41 and see what Jesus believed about Jonah. Jonah is mentioned in the most historically accurate book of the ancient world. (See 2 Kings 14:25.)

HOSEA: Hosea's love and restoration of his own sinful, adulterous wife is a picture of God's forgiving love for sinful Israel.

Chapters 1–3. Hosea's personal experience a picture of God's dealings with adulterous Israel.

Chapters 4–14. The earlier message given in greater detail.

AMOS: Amos preached that a nation is responsible for her national sins. The heathen nations surrounding God's people were condemned to judgment for their national sins, but Israel was condemned in even more severe terms for her sins since her light was greater.

THE PROPHETS TO THE KINGDOM OF JUDAH

(Listed in the probable order of their appearance)

JOEL: The country had been threatened with destruction because of devastating swarms of locusts and excessive drought. Though the plague was removed through fasting and prayer, it was made the basis for prophecy of a terrible day of final judgment for all nations. The faithful will be rewarded while evildoers will be punished.

ISAIAH: *(Read Isaiah 9:6–7; 53)*

Isaiah was a nobleman and prophet of Hezekiah's day who warned, comforted, and advised his rulers. He prophesied the captivity of Judah's kingdom but foretold the dawn of the new Kingdom. He prophesied both the sufferings and the glory of the coming Christ. Notice the many prophecies about Christ taken from Isaiah listed on page 63.

MICAH: Micah preached to the northern and southern kingdoms regarding coming judgment and future restoration and blessing. Chapters 1–3 show a dark picture, chapters 4–5 a bright one, chapter 6 contains more judgment, and from 7:7 on the book gives a glorious picture of Israel's future.

NAHUM: The doom of Ninevah, the capital of Assyria, is pronounced, explained and described by Nahum. The three chapters tell of Ninevah judged, sentenced and executed.

ZEPHANIAH: The Day of the Lord is stressed by Zephaniah. This day brings destruction to the false remnant of Baal (chapter 1), destroys the God-rejecting nations (2–3:7), and purifies and blesses the true remnant of God's people (3:8–20).

JEREMIAH: "The weeping prophet"

Jeremiah was from a priestly family. While still a boy he was called to be a prophet. For his loyalty in preaching God's word for half a century, he was despised, feared, hated, and persecuted. Because he predicted the overthrow of Jerusalem, and seventy years of captivity, he was called a traitor and thrown into a dungeon but was rescued by a friend at court.

LAMENTATIONS was written by Jeremiah as a poetic expression of his grief for the destruction and desolation of Jerusalem and the temple and for the captivity and miseries of the people.

HABAKKUK: Right will prevail. Judah was being punished by wicked Babylonians, but the Babylonians would in turn be punished.

OBADIAH: The Land of Edom will be judged for her mistreatment of God's people. Israel will be blessed.

PROPHECIES OF CHRIST IN THE PROPHETS

What event in the life of Christ is prophesied in each of the following verses?

Old Testament Reference	New Testament Fulfillment
Isa. 9:7 _____	Matt. 1:1
Mic. 5:2 _____	Matt. 2:1
Isa. 7:14 _____	Matt. 1:18
Hos. 11:1 _____	Matt. 2:14
Jer. 31:15 _____	Matt. 2:16–18
Mal. 3:1 _____	Mark 1:2, 4
Isa. 61:1, 2 _____	Luke 4:17–21
Zech. 9:9 _____	John 12:15
Zech. 11:12 _____	Matt. 26:15
Isa. 53:7 _____	Matt. 26:62–63
Isa. 50:6 _____	Mark 14:65
Isa. 53:4–5 _____	Matt. 8:16–17
Isa. 53:12 _____	Matt. 27:38
Zech. 12:10 _____	John 19:34
Isa. 53:9 _____	Matt. 27:56–60

THE CAPTIVITY

(Read Psalm 137)

THE KINGDOM OF ISRAEL was taken captive into Assyria in the northern part of the Euphrates-Tigris valley. *(Read 2 Kings 17:4–18)*

THE KINGDOM OF JUDAH was taken captive in three sections to Babylon in the southern part of the Euphrates-Tigris valley.

1. 605 BC Nebuchadnezzar carried away the princes (Daniel, etc.) and mighty men. (Read 2 Kings 24:11–16)
2. 598 BC Nebuchadnezzar took the king and many people to Babylon. (Read 2 Kings 25:1–7)
3. 587 BC Jerusalem and the temple were burned and destroyed and most of the remaining people taken to Babylon. *(Read 2 Kings 25:8–21)*
    Locate Assyria and Babylon on the map, page 13.

REASON FOR THE CAPTIVITY.

(Psalm 137 gives a picture of how the captives felt.)

Why do you think God allowed this to happen to His people?

_____

_____

BOOKS OF THE CAPTIVITY PERIOD

EZEKIEL: Ezekiel was taken to Babylon soon after Daniel. He prophesied the soon coming destruction of Jerusalem. His later visions were of the remnant returning, Jerusalem restored, the new temple, and the glorious kingdom to come.

DANIEL: *(Read Daniel 1–6)* Daniel was taken as a youth to Babylon where he lived during the 70-year period of the captivity. At times he occupied high offices in the Babylonian and Persian empires.

Give the main subject or subjects of each of the following chapters:

Daniel 1 _____

Daniel 2 _____

Daniel 3 _____

Daniel 4 _____

Daniel 5 _____

Daniel 6 _____

Daniel 7–12 relates other great prophetical visions.

After reading Daniel 1–6 give the most important things told about each of the following:

1. Daniel _____

    _____

2. Nebuchadnezzar _____

    _____

3. Shadrach, Meshach, and Abednego_____

    _____

4. Belshazzar _____

    _____

5. Darius _____

ESTHER

(Read Esther 1–10)

Esther lived during the captivity, 480 BC, under the reign of the Persian monarch Ahasuerus, the Xerxes of secular history.

1. *Identify the following:*
   a. Ahasuerus _____
   b. Vashti _____
   c. Esther _____
   d. Mordecai _____
   e. Haman _____

2. *Summarize the plot:* _____
   _____
   _____
   _____
   _____

3. *Answer the following:*
   a. Why is this story important in studying the line of the seed through which the Messiah is to come? _____
   _____
   _____

   b. What does the Jewish feast of Purim celebrate? _____
   _____

   c. The word "God" is not mentioned in Esther. Is the protective working of God shown in the book?_____

CHANGES DURING THE CAPTIVITY

1. The name **Jew** came into use not only applying to the people from Judah, but to all the Hebrews.

2. The **Samaritans** were people of mixed races and religions (partly Jewish) sent as colonists to Palestine from Assyria during Israel's captivity. *(See 2 Kings 17:24–34.)*

3. **Synagogues** were established as Jewish meeting places for worship and Scripture reading. The Israelites were far away from Jerusalem where the temple lay in ruins. During this time greater respect for the laws of Moses developed and sacred books became very important.

4. That God can be **worshiped anywhere** was a lesson learned when the temple was destroyed.

5. **Idolatry** was so cured in the Israelites that they never again showed a tendency to worship idols.

6. The **people's vision was enlarged** through learning the trades, customs, and languages of other people.

7. The **promises of the Messiah** became clearer and the desire for His coming increased.

THE RESTORATION OF THE JEWS

The restoration took place during the Persian rule and covered a period of about 100 years.

In the first 20 years (536–516 BC) Zerubbabel the governor and Joshua the priest led in rebuilding the temple.

Haggai and Zechariah prophesied.

In the last 25 years (457–432 BC) Ezra returned to teach the Law and Nehemiah rebuilt the walls of Jerusalem.

Malachi lived and prophesied at this time.

There were three returning groups of Jews.

I.   Under **Zerubbabel** in 536 BC about 50,000 returned. The **temple** was rebuilt.

II. Under **Ezra** in 457 BC about 6,000 returned. The **Scriptures** were taught.

III. **Nehemiah** and an army escort returned in 445 BC. The walls were rebuilt.

FIRST EXPEDITION

(Read Ezra 1; 3:8–13; 4:1–6, 17–24; 5:1–2; 6:15–22)

1. What Persian king wanted a house built for God in Jerusalem? (1) _____

2. A group spoken of in Ezra 9:8 as a "remnant" wanted to return to Jerusalem. What does this name indicate as to the proportion of Jews who returned? _____

3. How did the Jews remaining in Persia aid those who were returning? (1:4) _____
   _____

4. What special vessels were carried back? _____
   _____

5. *Read Psalm 126 as a picture of the joy of returning Jews.*

6. What various sounds were heard at the laying of the foundation of the temple? _____
   _____

7. What did the "adversaries" (Samaritans) do which caused the Jews to stop the building of the temple? (4) _____
   _____
   _____

8. Which prophets finally aroused the people to undertake again the rebuilding of the temple? (5:1–12)
   _____

9. What did Haggai say was the cause of their poor crops and pitiful state? (Read Haggai 1)
   _____
   _____

10. Under whose reign was the temple completed? (6:15) _____
    (Zerubbabel's temple was completed in 516 BC)

11. What famous feasts were celebrated? (6:19–22) _____

SECOND EXPEDITION

(Read Ezra 7:1–10; 8:21–36; 9:1–5; 10:1–17)

1. From what priestly tribe did Ezra descend? (7:1–5) _____

2. What was Ezra's office or occupation? (7:6) _____

3. Why did Ezra's group pray and fast before making the journey? (8:21–23) _____
   _____
   _____

4. How did Ezra make sure that all the gifts for the temple were brought safely to Jerusalem? (8:24–34)
    _____
    _____

5. What sin of the Israelites greatly disturbed Ezra? (9:1–5)_____

6. What difficult thing did the men do which showed they were truly repentant for their sin? (10:1–17)
    _____

Tradition states that Ezra and his associates collected and united all the Old Testament books into the Old Testament Canon or Scriptures.

THIRD EXPEDITION

(Read Nehemiah 1; 2; 4:1–9, 16–20; 8; 13:15–27)

1. *In reading watch for the times Nehemiah prayed and list them here:*
    _____
    _____

2. What did Nehemiah learn about the condition of Jerusalem?_____
    _____

3. What was Nehemiah's position in the Persian court? (1:11) _____

4. How did the king discover that Nehemiah wanted to return and help the Jews rebuild the walls of Jerusalem? (2:1–6)_____
    _____
    _____

5. What two men led the Samaritan enemies in opposing the Israelites in their work? (2:10, 19)
    _____

6. After glancing through Nehemiah 3 what would you say was the plan for the building of the walls? _____
    _____

7. What two things did the Samaritans do to hinder the building? (4:1–3; 4:7–8)_____
    _____

8. Why did the builders carry swords with them?_____
    _____

9. In how many days were the walls completed? (6:15) _____
    _____

10. Who brought great blessing to all the people through his public reading of the Scripture? (8)
    _____

11. On Nehemiah's return visit to Jerusalem what public sin did he strongly oppose? (13:15–22)
    _____

12. Why was intermarriage with other races so displeasing to God? (13:23–27) Read also 2 Corinthians 6:14 _____
    _____
    _____

PROPHETS OF THE RESTORATION

HAGGAI: The unfinished temple of the restoration.
ZECHARIAH: The coming of the Lord.
MALACHI: The final message to a disobedient nation.
   After Malachi's prophecies ceased the Bible has an inter-testament period of 400 years before the silence is broken and the glorious events of the New Testament begin.

MORE TIME TO TEACH WHAT MATTERS MOST

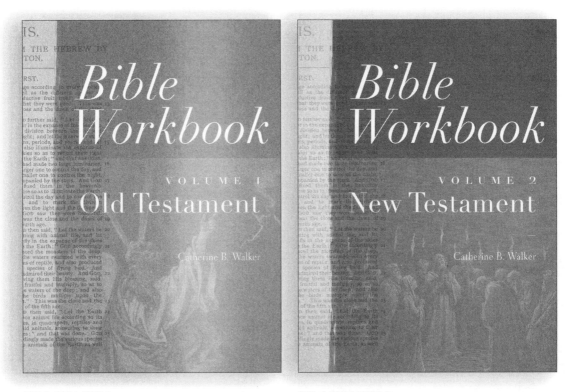

978-0-8024-0751-1

978-0-8024-0752-8

The workbooks are full of exercises, questions, and maps that ensure students have the fundamentals down before you teach. Each workbook contains thousands of fill-in-the-blank questions as well as diagrams and maps students interact with. They can be adapted for virtually any teaching setting (homeschool, Bible class, adult Sunday school).

also available as eBooks

STUDY THE BIBLE WITH PROFESSORS FROM MOODY BIBLE INSTITUTE

THE BEST ALLEGORY EVER WRITTEN